First World War
and Army of Occupation
War Diary
France, Belgium and Germany

32 DIVISION
Headquarters, Branches and Services
Royal Army Veterinary Corps
Assistant Director Veterinary Services
21 November 1915 - 7 December 1919

WO95/2379/4

The Naval & Military Press Ltd
www.nmarchive.com
Published in association with The National Archives

Published by

The Naval & Military Press Ltd

Unit 10 Ridgewood Industrial Park,

Uckfield, East Sussex,

TN22 5QE England

Tel: +44 (0) 1825 749494

www.naval-military-press.com

www.nmarchive.com

This diary has been reprinted in facsimile from the original. Any imperfections are inevitably reproduced and the quality may fall short of modern type and cartographic standards.

© **Crown Copyright**
Images reproduced by permission of The National Archives, London, England, 2015.

Contents

Document type	Place/Title	Date From	Date To
Heading	WO95/2379/3		
Heading	32nd Division Divl Troops Asst Dir. Vety Services Nov 1915-1919 Dec.		
Heading	A.D.V.S. 32nd Div. Vol: I		
War Diary	Havre Ailly Le Hant Clocher	21/11/1915	28/11/1915
War Diary	Flesselles	29/11/1915	31/12/1915
Heading	A.D.V.S. 32nd Div. Vol: 2		
War Diary	Flesselles	01/01/1916	02/01/1916
War Diary	Senlis	03/01/1916	13/02/1916
War Diary	Henencourt	14/02/1916	29/02/1916
Heading	ADVS 32nd Div. Vol 4		
War Diary	Henencourt	01/03/1916	30/04/1916
War Diary	Senlis	01/05/1916	30/06/1916
Heading	War Diary Of A.D.V.S. 32nd Division Volume VIII From July 1st 1916 To July 31st 1916		
War Diary	Senlis	01/07/1916	04/07/1916
War Diary	Contay	05/07/1916	08/07/1916
War Diary	Warloy	09/07/1916	13/07/1916
War Diary	Bouzincourt	14/07/1916	16/07/1916
War Diary	Beauval	16/07/1916	17/07/1916
War Diary	Doullens	18/07/1916	19/07/1916
War Diary	Flers	20/07/1916	20/07/1916
War Diary	Bryas	21/07/1916	21/07/1916
War Diary	Lillers	22/07/1916	26/07/1916
War Diary	Bethune	27/07/1916	31/07/1916
Heading	War Diary Of A.D.V.S. 32nd Div. From Aug. 1st To Aug. 31st 16. Vol 9		
War Diary	Bethune	01/08/1916	31/08/1916
Heading	War Diary Of A.D.V.S. 32nd Div. From Sept 1st To Sept 30th 1916 Vol X.		
War Diary	Bethune	01/09/1916	16/10/1916
War Diary	Chelers	17/10/1916	17/10/1916
War Diary	Le Couroy	18/10/1916	18/10/1916
War Diary	Beauval	19/10/1916	21/10/1916
War Diary	Contay	22/10/1916	23/10/1916
War Diary	Bouzincourt	24/10/1916	17/11/1916
War Diary	Bertrancourt	18/11/1916	25/11/1916
War Diary	Doullens Canaples	26/11/1916	30/11/1916
Heading	War Diary Of A.D.V.S. 32nd Div. From 1st Dec. 1916 To 31st Dec 16 Vol. XII.		
War Diary	Canaples	01/12/1916	31/12/1916
Heading	War Diary Of A.D.V.S. 32nd Division From 1st Of January To 31st January 1917 Vol. No. 14		
War Diary	Canaples	01/01/1917	06/01/1917
War Diary	Marieux	07/01/1917	09/01/1917
War Diary	Bus	10/01/1917	23/01/1917
War Diary	Bertrancourt	24/01/1917	31/01/1917
Miscellaneous	D.A.G. 3rd Echelon	15/03/1917	15/03/1917
Heading	War Diary Of A.D.V.S. 32nd Div. From 1st Feby 17 To 28th Feby 1917 Vol XV.		

War Diary	Bertrancourt	01/02/1917	17/02/1917
War Diary	Villers	18/02/1917	18/02/1917
War Diary	Bocage	18/02/1917	28/02/1917
Heading	War Diary Of A.D.V.S. 32nd Division From 1st March To 31st March 1917. Vol. XVI.		
War Diary	Quesnel	01/03/1917	17/03/1917
War Diary	Quesnel	18/03/1917	18/03/1917
War Diary	Warvillers	18/03/1917	19/03/1917
War Diary	Leancourt	20/03/1917	20/03/1917
War Diary	Nesle	21/03/1917	29/03/1917
War Diary	Auroir	30/03/1917	31/03/1917
Heading	War Diary Of A.D.V.S. 32nd Division From April 1st To April 30th 1917 (Vol XVII)		
War Diary	Auroir	01/04/1917	21/04/1917
War Diary	Voyenne	22/04/1917	30/04/1917
Heading	War Diary Of A.D.V.S. 32nd Division From May 1st 1917 To May 31st 1917 Vol. XVIII		
War Diary	Voyenne	01/05/1917	16/05/1917
War Diary	Beaucourt	17/05/1917	31/05/1917
Heading	War Diary Of A.D.V.S., 32nd Division From 1st June To 30th June 1917. (Volume XIX).		
War Diary	Beaucourt	01/06/1917	02/06/1917
War Diary	Vieux Berquin	02/06/1917	14/06/1917
War Diary	Coxide Les Brains	15/06/1917	20/06/1917
War Diary	Coxide Les Bains	21/06/1917	30/06/1917
Heading	War Diary Of D.A.D.V.S. 32nd Div. From July 1st-July 31st 17. Vol 20		
War Diary	Coxide Les Bains	01/07/1917	19/07/1917
War Diary	Rosendale	20/07/1917	31/07/1917
Heading	War Diary Of D.A.D.V.S. 32nd Div. From 1st Aug. To 31st Aug 1917. Vol 21		
War Diary	Rosendale	01/08/1917	03/08/1917
War Diary	Coxyde Les Bains	04/08/1917	18/08/1917
War Diary	La-Panne	19/08/1917	28/08/1917
War Diary	Coxyde-Les-Bains	29/08/1917	31/08/1917
Heading	War Diary Of D.A.D.V.S. 32nd Division From Sept 1st To Sept 30/17. (Volume XXII).		
War Diary	Coxyde Les Bains	01/09/1917	30/09/1917
Heading	War Diary Of D.A.D.V.S. 32nd Division From 1st To 31st October 1917. Volume XXIII.		
War Diary	Coxyde Les Bains	01/10/1917	06/10/1917
War Diary	Arras	07/10/1917	08/10/1917
War Diary	Coxyde	09/10/1917	10/10/1917
War Diary	La Panne	11/10/1917	11/10/1917
War Diary	Rosendale	12/10/1917	23/10/1917
War Diary	Le Clipon	24/10/1917	26/10/1917
War Diary	Lederzele	27/10/1917	31/10/1917
Heading	War Diary Of D.A.D.V.S. 32nd Div. From 1st-30th Nov. 1917. Vol 25		
War Diary	Lederzele	01/11/1917	11/11/1917
War Diary	Poperinghe	12/11/1917	24/11/1917
War Diary	Brake Camp	24/11/1917	30/11/1917
Heading	War Diary Of D.A.D.V.S. 32nd Division From Dec. 1st To Dec. 31st 1917 (Volume XXV).		
War Diary	Brake Camp	01/12/1917	30/12/1917
War Diary	Zutkerque	30/12/1917	31/12/1917

Heading	War Diary Of D.A.D.V.S. 32nd Division From January 1st To Janry 31st 1918. (Volume XXVI).		
War Diary	Zutkerque	01/01/1918	30/01/1918
War Diary	Elverdinghe	31/01/1918	31/01/1918
Heading	War Diary Of D.A.D.V.S. 32nd Division From Feb 1st To 28th 1918 (Volume XXVIII).		
War Diary	Elverdinghe	01/02/1918	28/02/1918
Heading	War Diary Of D.A.D.V.S. 32nd Division From Mar 1st To Mar 31st 1918. (Volume 29).		
War Diary	Elverdinghe	01/03/1918	28/03/1918
War Diary	Hermaville	29/03/1918	31/03/1918
Heading	War Diary Of D.A.D.V.S. 32nd Div. From 1st April To 30th April 1918 (Volume 28).		
War Diary	Hermaville	01/04/1918	01/04/1918
War Diary	Humber Camp	02/04/1918	05/04/1918
War Diary	Mondicourt	06/04/1918	25/04/1918
War Diary	Bavincourt	26/04/1918	30/04/1918
Heading	War Diary of D.A.D.V.S., 32nd Division From May 1st To May 31st 1918 (Volume 30).		
War Diary	Bavelincourt	01/05/1918	31/05/1918
Heading	War Diary Of D.A.D.V.S. 32nd Division From June 1st To June 30th 1918 (Volume 31).		
War Diary	Bavincourt	01/06/1918	30/06/1918
Heading	War Diary Of D.A.D.V.S. 32nd Division From July 1st To July 31st 1918. (Volume 32).		
War Diary	Bavincourt	01/07/1918	19/07/1918
War Diary	Bambecque	20/07/1918	31/07/1918
Heading	War Diary Of D.A.D.V.S. 32nd Division From Aug 1st To Aug 31st 1918 (Volume 33).		
War Diary	Bambecque	01/08/1918	07/08/1918
War Diary	Cavillon	08/08/1918	10/08/1918
War Diary	Cagny	11/08/1918	19/08/1918
War Diary	Villers Brettoneux	20/08/1918	24/08/1918
War Diary	Bayonvillers	25/08/1918	31/08/1918
Heading	War Diary Of D.A.D.V.S. 32nd Division From 1st To 30th Sept 1918 (Volume 34).		
War Diary	Bayonvillers	01/09/1918	04/09/1918
War Diary	Luarry	05/09/1918	08/09/1918
War Diary	Misery	09/09/1918	14/09/1918
War Diary	Fouilloy	14/09/1918	19/09/1918
War Diary	Corbie	20/09/1918	23/09/1918
War Diary	Bouvincourt	24/09/1918	30/09/1918
Heading	War Diary Of D.A.D.V.S. 32nd Division From Oct 1st To 31st 1918 (Volume 35).		
War Diary	Bouzincourt	01/10/1918	06/10/1918
War Diary	Catelet	07/10/1918	20/10/1918
War Diary	Bohain	21/10/1918	31/10/1918
Heading	War Diary Of D.A.D.V.S. 32nd Division From 1st To 30th November 1918 (Volume 36).		
War Diary	Busigny	01/11/1918	06/11/1918
War Diary	Bazuel	07/11/1918	07/11/1918
War Diary	Favril	08/11/1918	09/11/1918
War Diary	Gd Fayt	10/11/1918	12/11/1918
War Diary	Avesnes	13/11/1918	14/11/1918
War Diary	Sains Du Nord	15/11/1918	19/11/1918
War Diary	Sivry	20/11/1918	20/11/1918

War Diary	Rance	21/11/1918	30/11/1918
War Diary	Bioul	13/12/1918	31/12/1918
Heading	Lancashire Division (Late 32nd Divn) D.A. Dir. Vety Serv. Jan-Dec. D.A.D.V.S. Jan-Nov.		
Heading	War Diary Of D.A.D.V.S. 32nd Division From Janry. 1st To 31st 1919 (Volume 38)		
War Diary	Bioul	01/01/1919	31/01/1919
Heading	War Diary Of D.A.D.V.S. 32nd Division From 1st To 28th February 1919 (Volume 39).		
War Diary	Bioul	01/02/1919	01/02/1919
War Diary	Bonne	02/02/1919	28/02/1919
Heading	War Diary Of D.A.D.V.S. Lancashire Division From Mar 1st To 31st 1919 (Volume 40).		
War Diary	Bonn	01/03/1919	31/03/1919
Heading	War Diary of D.A.D.V.S. Lancashire Division From April 1st to April 30th 1919 (Volume 41.)		
War Diary	Bonn	21/04/1919	30/04/1919
War Diary	Bonn	01/04/1919	20/04/1919
Heading	War Diary of D.A.D.V.S. Lancashire Division From May 1st to 31st 1919 (Volume 42)		
War Diary	Bonn	01/05/1919	31/05/1919
Heading	War Diary of D.A.D.V.S. Lancashire Division From June 1st 1919 to 30th 1919 (Volume 43).		
War Diary		01/06/1919	30/06/1919
Heading	War Diary D.A.D.V.S. Lancashire Division From July 1st 1919 To 31st 1919 (Volume 44)		
War Diary	Bonn	01/07/1919	31/07/1919
Heading	War Diary Of D.A.D.V.S. Lancashire Division From Aug. 1st To 31st 1919 (Volume 45).		
War Diary	Bonn	01/08/1919	30/09/1919
Miscellaneous	A.A. & QMG Lancs Divn.	05/11/1919	05/11/1919
War Diary	Bonn	01/10/1919	07/12/1919

WD 995/2379(3)

WD 957/2379(3)

32ND DIVISION
DIVL TROOPS

ASST DIR. VETY SERVICES
NOV 1915-DEC 1918
1919 ~~NOV~~ DEC

Add. 32935.
Vol: II

121/4935

Nov 15
Dec 18

WAR DIARY or INTELLIGENCE SUMMARY

Army Form C. 2118

of A.D.V.S. 32nd Div.

(Erase heading not required.)

Place	Date	Hour	Summary of Events and Information	Remarks and references to Appendices
HAVRE ALLY to Havre Oct.	Nov 21/15	7 a.m.	Arrived after a very good journey from SOUTHAMPTON. There were no casualties of any sort. There was been with us in England. Left at 11 am. G.R-M.	
	22nd	3 p.m.	13 horses in the 95th Inf Brigade got left behind in the truck as the train had stopped 3 times. The 3 horses gun in board the 4 horses, but the thunderous noise on the middle between the 2 others. We arrived at PONT REMY at 11 & m & reached our billets. I went to see the O.C. Sen. Train as	
"	23rd		I heard that he had not got a P.O. G.R-M. I went to the Head Quarters of No. 53rd Field Artillery & got the names of their O.O. No O.C Res. arrangements in a mess anywhere. Up to the 15th December an 18 pr. I went to the P.O. T.O. REMY Station to see an inquiry. There is No ammunition and got a written report had I proceeded toward till the next day. I reported an arrival to reference to the ADVS 3rd army R-M. I went to the Station. I found the above horse was dead. I met the Veterinaire ADC at the	
"	24th		sitting up what I could arrange and with the Hotel Proprietor to stabling police at the stopped. In the afternoon I motored to ABBEVILLE to see Major OLIVER. If I could send supplies to No. 5 Vety Hosp. G.R-M.	
"	25th	10 a.m.	I went to A.3.C & inspected the horses belonging to ADVS 3rd Div. also the animals of was a.o.m. a train in A.3.C. I inspected all the animals in the Gen. Signal Co. G.R.M.	
"	26th	2 p.m.	AVC came to see me and the 4th Div. & inspected all the animals in the Gun. Signal Co. had quite found all the animals in the Pioneer Battalion & gave out Camel Hair Brushes to some	
		10 a.m	I went found an old Field Ambulance ADC when I went to ROSEROSE of BARTRUM A.V.C. to BOUCHON	
		2 pm	I went to LONG & our Pol Ambulance A.V.C. & worth his Mobile Vety Section arrived. G.R-M. Present	
"	27th	10 a.m	Lt. Col. GIBSON A.V.C. Lt. MILLS A.V.C. with his Mobile Vety about them to MI Hosp ABBEVILLE.	
		10 a.m	Lt. MILLS went to the A.S.C. as he had 10 horses & mules about the Pont du Sous animals & found Pneumonia. G.R-M.	
"	28th		Field office with all the 4th Div. Sgt to FLESSELLES & arranged thereat. G-30	
		10 am	I found our Field Ambulance to inform them that the east Inf Brigade here sent a P.O. to apply for the	
FLES- SELLES	29th		A.S.C. & Field Ambulances. Assistance. G.R.M.	
	30th		It they so has any Vety assistance. In the afternoon I went unaccompanied the animals & Mules at rest. Lt. Anderson A.V.C came.	
		10 am	The A.D.V.S. 3rd Corps came to see me. For 3 animals to be sent to the M.V. Section. G.R.M.	
	Dec 1		Ambulance & gave instructions. In the afternoon the 97th Inf Brigade G.R.M.	
			Case was supplied that he that & Unknown which ND had taken to be dialed & lost after the D.A.E. who said	
			that MAJor R.A. Johnston. A sight down & lived with me to see the 8 A.C. returned. Veterinary Supervision very badly. Joined the main at various whether the 8 horses left behind by the 95	
			Informed 2nd Div. collected the bodies to see to for the permissing. G.R.M.	

WAR DIARY of A.D.V.S. 32nd Division

INTELLIGENCE SUMMARY

Army Form C. 2118

Place	Date	Hour	Summary of Events and Information	Remarks and references to Appendices
FLESSELLES	Dec. 1st	9 a.m.	Went to see Lt. DRINKWATER a/y C. of Lt. WYNNE WILLIAMS of ST SAUVEUR. The Lafter reported sore the death of a mule left behind by 2nd D.A.C. I went to see the mule, but he knew nothing about it. Inspected the case of the D.A.V.S. 3rd Army. Arranged for all to pick up cases to the M.V.S. every morning to be dressed.	
"	2nd	9 a.m.	Went to D.A.D.S. about getting lamps for long jobs to no avail. In the afternoon I motored to YAUCHELLE & saw S. VS & everything in very good order.	
"	3rd		Motoring on to SarCamp I left a man at A.V.S. at SUR CAMPS for the night. Received wire from D.V.S. asking one of them to animals evacuated by Vauchelle.	
"	4th		M.V.L.S. a V.S. the 28 Light dungs neglected 3690e- Lieuenant 6 years old 4½-2. I spent the day in the morning and although a thorough Enquiry into the above I am in the afternoon I went to see the D C 110? Vets Hosp. at then the D.V.S. C who gave me an interview to find out officers horse far furnished a J.R.M. I inspected the animals of Al. KING WELL Two green Surgical cases behind the C. not say that. That the was seriously Retained in the Evening. J.R.M. a wound inside of near fore arm. I made out weakly Return.	
"	5th		Went to the CHESHIRE Brigade & after thoroughly investigating the case came to the conclusion that the Glanders case was not the animal which was suffered to A. KING WELL Champaign who was collected at BOUCHON in a float on 28 Nov. & told by the WEL SH HOW. to be collected. Must also enquire into this affair. Sent to A.D.S. 3rd Army a / the O.C. Dvs Hosp. by Brigadier. Motor there ambulance Glanders Bvy. who left me alter interview. I went to see Lt. GIBSON a V.S. & to the Vet Van Lance in Shipping. I sent the 10 cases to casting 9.30 a.m. In the aft. I motored to BOUCHON & thoroughly disinfected (by spraying) the stable where the Glanders case had been & I went to see A.D.M.S. 36 Div. L. Co. then to A.D.V.S.	
"	7th		Rest day. J.R.M. A.D.V.S. came to see me & made arrangements for settling the q Welsh How. Bright work mallein. In the evening I motored to ALBERVILLE & got the mallein from R.M. Brigade.	
"	8th		Started with Lt. J of the other Btn. Ord 364 tesied up the 3 animals of H How. Brigade. In the afternoon I inspected the A.S.C. Co horses the animals of the 1st Bordsman other Bvd 9½. Inf Brigade. SR-m.	
"	9th		About 11 a.m. P. YOU! RE Jo pce ome car Lt BARTRUM a v.c. wanted to show me. Glanders & all the horse in the area M. WELSH HOW Brigade & one don't doubt. Some could not fire drawn & D. v.s. informed	

WAR DIARY of A.D.V.S. 32nd Div.

Army Form C. 2118

INTELLIGENCE SUMMARY
(Erase heading not required.)

Instructions regarding War Diaries and Intelligence Summaries are contained in F.S. Regs., Part II. and the Staff Manual respectively. Title Pages will be prepared in manuscript.

Place	Date	Hour	Summary of Events and Information	Remarks and references to Appendices
FLES-SELLES	13th		Went to gain knowledge of the WELSH DIV. Brigade. Could not find any transport. She went to join the BARTRUM D.V.C. Then went to inspect all the horses of the 96th Inf. Bgde. & 97 Fld Ambulance & the M.V. Section & found all in good order. Inspected weekly Returns. etc.	
	14th		Visited the Horses were sent to the B.O.P & 5 sore bks. Dr 32nd Div. sent in a Report on available forage to make Sheds to be made. G.R.M.	
			Rejoined 12 ambulance horses in 97 Div. the 1/1 WELSH Fd. Bgde. G.R.M.	
	15th		Inspected all the horses in 96 Brigade & Signal Co. Shoeing very bad. Inspected the animals in the D.A.C. Inspected all the horses of the 1/1 De Co. A.S.C. & the wagons, Horses Shoes in fair order. Was angry with him also G.R.M.	
	16th		Visited 97 Nose Bags & looked about men who use unsrupd Curbs in Shoring to give every chance of freedom. G.R.M.	
			Inspected the mules & pack of the horses in 2 Nor Dir.) of the 219 & K.S. with the Conception of 6 then our Division was good but the Shoring very disgraceful & also office work and tho. 6th making orderly the A.C. Stonemaghers horses 13 animals having sore shins etc. Sent in Report to the D.D.V.S. Found the animals working well. Their full allowance of the 96 Fd Ambulance not being drawn. Passenger ambulance. G.R.M.	
	17th		Horses not being drawn. In the afternoon I inspected the Horses of the 95 Feld Amb. & 204 to employ the Div g. Sergt of A.S.C. Stonemaghers the 2 Battalions of the Brigade & to effect the Horses of the 96th morning already into a long column and shall Captain of the 3 gas office work all the morning. I inspected the Horses of the 95 Fd Amb. & 204 Infantry Brigade. In the afternoon I inspected the Horses of the 96 Feld Amb. & 204 C.A.S.C. found not in the correct amount of forage was not being drawn supplies to A.S.C. of any for their. Sent in the number of Horses to many think smaller than some to the O.C. Div. Train Ration. G.R.M.	
	18th		To Draw the 19th Div. Corn Ration. G.R.M. Champion Shire & Heavy draft on the 96th Inf. Brigade, Pioneer Battalion of 91st Field Ambulance Sent in Cheques to the various Units. G.R.M. Sent relieving tackle on the 95 Inf. Bgde. & L/Cpl ANDERSON A.V.C. took dungworld stair & turned to join half the Sink. G.R.M.	
	19th		Made out weekly Returns. Made out Report on fall Ammo. Reports from V.Q's in Nottingham Equipment about knife Canteen Horses had done their work with the D.A. 2 M.G. G.R.M.	

WAR DIARY

INTELLIGENCE SUMMARY

(Erase heading not required.)

Army Form C. 2118

Place	Date	Hour	Summary of Events and Information	Remarks and references to Appendices
FLES SELLES	Dec. 20th 21st		I went to SEMLIS to see the A.D.V.S. 51st Div. Then went on horseback to the lines on the Belgian Borders. I sent Camel-hair Brushes to the 90th Inf. Brigade. G.R-M.	
	22nd		Attended H.Q.C.'s Conference at 9-30. I tested with 2V.Os two Batteries of the 94th & CHESHIRE Brigade & in the afternoon the H.Q. Co. A.S.C. at ST VAASSE. G.R-M. I/DRINKWATER, Pt BARTRUM A/V.C. & I tested the animals of the D.A.C. & the 1/4th WELSH Brigade. I went & inspected all the horses tested the Jas Lytre. I found the D.A.C. had not got any nose-bags for their mules. I went & saw D.A.D.O.S. on my return & the nose-bags were to D.A.C. to-day & new-days following. G.R-M.	
	23rd		I tested with Malin Horsemann 2 Batteries of the CHESHIRE Brigade & the stable of the 1/9/2nd WELSH Brigade. Then I went & examined the Horses which had been tested. The 2 French horses (q?) I could not find any reaction. G.R-M.	
	24th		I inspected the 2 Bartemis horses the Jay before also the 2 mules. No reactors. Then I saw the Horses of 2. S.C. I found that no Nose-bags had yet been issued out to the mules and D.A.C. I went again to inspect the horsed animals of the D.A.C. as there was rather suspicious case. Our him turned to be a Non-Reactor. I found out that the mules were only being fed on hay with own arrive on arrived. G.R-M.	
	25th		I then saw 2 mules left behind by D.C. Then I inspected the pick in Head quarter Co. A.S.C. I then went to see the DRINKWATER 2 BRTRUM & arranged for the Transhorn of their horses which would be unfit to travel the next day. G.R-M. 89 animals were evacuated to no 5 Vy Hosp.	
	26th		To see WELSH Artillery Off Kin Simson.	
	29th		I am very sorry to lose no V.Os as they were all exceptionally nice fellows and very reliable. G.R-M.	

WAR DIARY
or
INTELLIGENCE SUMMARY

(Erase heading not required.)

Army Form C. 2118

Place	Date	Hour	Summary of Events and Information	Remarks and references to Appendices
FLES-SELLES	Dec 28th		Inspected the horses of the 92nd Field Ambulance. Stabling arrangements & horse Markings is some too good. Received a wire to go & see a horse in AMIENS belonging to the 53rd WELSH Artillery & went & found that it had arrived & gone. J.R.M. I bought 6 teams with or Arneffair & trucks. J.R.M.	
	29th		Took sick an officers charger with very badly broken knees. the 15 & 3rd Inf. Brigades the other week. He a 5.r.s. 37 & Brig. came over to see me & J. however him round. J.R.M.	
	30th		Went to visit the Sick in the 15 & 3rd Inf. Brigade. In the aft I went to TALMA to see the 27 & Brig. train. J.R.M.	
	31st		In the morning I read a new American Book called The Treatment of Wounds. In the afternoon I went to see the 15 & 3rd Inf. Brigade & from there into a Broken Rag was go to work. Then on to see the pick in its stead & washer Co a.S.C. J.R.M.	

Army Form C. 2118

WAR DIARY of A.D.V.S. 32nd Division

INTELLIGENCE SUMMARY

(Erase heading not required.)

Instructions regarding War Diaries and Intelligence Summaries are contained in F.S. Regs., Part II. and the Staff Manual respectively. Title Pages will be prepared in manuscript.

Place	Date	Hour	Summary of Events and Information	Remarks, and references to Appendices
FLESSELLES	Jany 1st		Inspected the horses of the 27th Div. Transport made out monthly Returns. J.R-M.	
"	2nd		Met the A.D.V.S. 5th Div. I handed over to him. J. left for SE No 15. J.R-M.	
"	3rd	3.30	Inspected the horses of the 92nd Field Ambulance & found everything in good order.	
	4th		Inspected the farm at CONTAY where the Mobile Vety. Section was going into billets. The Divisional A.V.C. attached J.R-M.	
			I saw all the pick in Head Quarters & Signal Co. J.R-M.	
			Went to MARTINSART & saw the Brigade Major 96th Inf. Brig. & the Sgt. A.V.C. attached. Also inspected all the many horses abt the O.C. 219 Co R.E. & 17th Nor'humberland Fusiliers. Obt a ✓ on Inspection. JR-M	
"	5th		At the A.S.C. all the 97th Inf. Brigade Transport. Inspected at 3.30 the M.V. Section. JR-M. Pick in the 14th "Reserve Park at ST. GRATIEN" and in afternoon the Signal Co. & J.R.M.	
"	6th		Inspected the horses in the 14th Reserve Park at ST. GRATIEN. J.R-M. 2nd Batt Innerskilling Fusiliers. J.R-M.	
"	7th		Visited the animals in the 19th Lane Fusiliers with Mallein - saw the pick in the Head quarters R.E. in the afternoon. J.R-M.	
"	8th		Inspected the animals in the 19th Lane Fusiliers at 9 & at 11 I looked & 2 of the animals of the 2 — Battalion Innerskilling Fusiliers at 2-30. Inspected the M.V.S. 5.12-M.	
			At 9 I went to ST. GRATIEN & looked with Mallein 139 horses in the 14th Reserve Park.	
"	9th		At 3 Inspected the Pigeons - the animals in 19th Lane Fusiliers & Innerskilling Fusiliers. J.R-M.	
			Went to QUERRIEUX & saw the horses of 70th Corp. Head Quarters.	
			Total 78 Horses in the 3rd Bridging train at last 2-30 I examined all the Eyes in the 16th Reserve PK. J.R.M.	
"	10th		I went to ST. GRATIEN & examined all the Eyes in the 14th Reserve Park - about 32 mules.	
"	11th		At 2 I went & saw all the animals in the 28th & examined the Eyes of the Innerskilling Fusiliers. J.R-M.	
			At 3 Inspected the M.V.S. & found all in good order. at 3 looked the roads of the animals in horsemilling.	
			Inspected the M.V.S. & J. R-M.	
"	12th		At 5-30 Attended G.O.C. Conference. J.R-M.	
			Examined the Eyes of Animals stabled on the Innerskilling Fusiliers. Inspected all the animals in the D.A.C. & the pick in B.Battery 20th Brigade & A.A. Battery, 160th Brig R.G.A. J.R-M	
"	13th		At 9-20 Inspected the horses of 5th Dragon Guards Battery now on M.Y.S. & then O.C. I red arranged and C.R.C. Tin roofing for his Stables. Then to inspect the pick in the 16th Heavy Bry. R.G.A. Like Innerskilling Fusiliers. J.R-M.	
"	14th		Inspected the 4 Batteries of the 161st Brig. R.F.A. Conference of J.R-M. the afternoon & J.R-M.	
"	15th		Looked with Mallein the 4 Batteries 161st Brigade. Also the 3rd Bridging train. J.R-M.	

Army Form C. 2118

WAR DIARY of A.D.V.S. 32nd Division

INTELLIGENCE SUMMARY

(Erase heading not required.)

Instructions regarding War Diaries and Intelligence Summaries are contained in F.S. Regs., Part II. and the Staff Manual respectively. Title Pages will be prepared in manuscript.

Place	Date	Hour	Summary of Events and Information	Remarks and references to Appendices
SEMLIS	Jan 9/16		Inspected horses of 161st Bry. R.F.A. Brig. V.O. frequently looked with mallein. At 3 I went to see a doubtful reactor in 174th Bty. R.F.A. I called to see Lt. Flanagan A.V.C. at 10-30 & found that he was not yet dressed. G.R-M.	
"	17th		Went to report against the posting of Mr Seaton. G.R-M.	
"	18th		Inspected the 161st Brigade for 2nd day. G.R-M.	
"			I helped to test 361 animals in the B.A.C.	
"	19th		Went at 3-30 to inspect a suspicious case of Glanders. G.R-M.	
"			I went to see the suspicious Glanders case of Syphitery & then on to the L.A.C.	
"			Then on to the 14th Reserve Park & inspected all the horses & evacuated 6 others on to Corp TR.M. case. G.R-M.	
"	20th		Inspected the tested animals in the B.A.C. & then went to make a P.M. on the I entered horse.	
"			Lt. D.V. Read A.V.C. arrived & I motored him to MERICOURT Station to get his kit & then took him to Corp T.R.M. G.R-M.	
"	21st		Lts. SMITH, FLANAGAN & I tested with mallein 310 animals in the B.A.C. G.R-M.	
"			All V.Os in this Division came to my office for a conference. G.R-M.	
"	22nd		Went to the stable of Glanders horse to see about disinfection &c, then on & inspected the horses	
"	23rd		I helped to test the 92nd Field Ambulance horses. G.R-M.	
"			animals in B.A.C. & arranged about the shoeing & forge tools. G.R-M.	
"			I selected some doubtful reactors in the M.A.C. at 2 I went & inspected the doubtful	
"	24th		I wrote out report re the Glanders case & met the D.D.V.S. on the 53rd WELSH artillery. G.R-M.	
"			reception B.A.C. & then on to test the infected 129 horses on also the Artillery of 3rd Div. G.R.-M.	
"	25th		I went to inspect the retested animals in B.A.C. & also the one in the Artillery of 3rd Div. G.R-M.	
"	26th		Office all day. G.R-M.	
"	27th		I helped to test the mobile of the 155th Brigade R.F.A. G.R-M.	
"	28th		Inspected all the horses of the 155th Brigade R.F.A. G.R-M.	
"	29th		Inspected all the horses of the 155th Brigade R.F.A. with mallein G.R-M.	
"	30th		Went the V.O. about testing the 161st & 162nd Brigade & 161st Brigade. G.R-M.	
"	31st		Inspected all the horses in the 161st & 162nd Brigade R.F.A. & Lt. Mills & then went on to examine the 164th Brigade & B.A.C. 161st Resting No. 168 B.Brigade R.F.A. I attended the L.O.C's conference. G.R-M. at 5-30 p.m.	

Graham Rees Mogg
Major
A.D.V.S. 32nd Div.

WAR DIARY of A.D.V.S. 32nd Div.

INTELLIGENCE SUMMARY

Army Form C. 2118

Instructions regarding War Diaries and Intelligence Summaries are contained in F.S. Regs., Part II. and the Staff Manual respectively. Title Pages will be prepared in manuscript.

(Erase heading not required.)

Place	Date	Hour	Summary of Events and Information	Remarks and references to Appendices
BEHENCOURT	July 1st		I examined horses previously tested in 168th 63 Brigade & also in 155th & Brigade R.F.A. I went to HENENCOURT to see about the Water Supply. J. R-m.	
	2nd		I went to inspect the 168th Brigade & found that Lt FLANAGAN knew nothing about his cases & that they were being very neglected. I inspected the M.V.S. J. R-m.	
	3rd		I inspected all the sick in the 168th 63 Brigade & found many very neglected. J. R-m.	
	4th		I inspected the animals in the Sick Lines. J. R-m.	
	5th		I saw L/FLANAGAN hand over the sick in 164th Brigade to L/REED. I inspected the M.V. Section from A.V.C. hand & set in the Div. train & the working of a Special Forge. J. R-m.	
	6th		I inspected orders on L/FLANAGAN A.V.C. J. R-m.	
	7th		I cast animals in the Divn. on the 161st & 168th Brigades R. F. A. & D.V.S. came to see me. J. R-m.	
	8th		Office all day. J. R-m.	
	9th		I started the V.O.p. testing the remaining animals in the R.A. I inspected the M. in V.S. & had 3 horses destroyed. In the afternoon I inspected the Stables & the Section of the 161st Bing & the Section of the Govnt. Pack. I went on to Flanagan & gave him a copy in Capt. Millys' Presence. J. R-m.	
	10th		I inspected the horses prepared for casting in the 155th & 164th Brigades & also one resided in Mallen. J. R-m.	
	11th		I also the 161st & 168th Brigades. J. R-m.	
	12th		I saw around the eyes of the V.O.p R. A. & then to Inspect the proposed Cookers in A.C. I gave a lecture to all the Surgts at V.O. J. R-m.	
	13th		I inspected the eyes of the Divn. R.A. A conference of V.Op in the afternoon. J. R-m.	
HENENCOURT	14th		HQrs moved to HENENCOURT. J. R-m.	
	15th		I inspected the Animals in the 17th Battn. R.I. just lodes with Mallen.	
	16th		I inspected all the animals in the 17th Battn. R.I. J. R-m.	
	17th		I inspected all the animals in the 17th Battn. of I found none had heated. V.Op came. I inspected the M. & S. & the animals prepared for Cooking on the 164th & 3 2. C. J. R-m.	
	18th		Office all day making out Mallen Returns. J. R-m.	
	19th		Office all the morning. In afternoon I went to ascertain about a supposed Contagious Disease at BEAUCOURT. J. R-m.	

Army Form C. 2118

WAR DIARY of A.D.V.S. 32nd Div.

INTELLIGENCE SUMMARY

(Erase heading not required.)

Instructions regarding War Diaries and Intelligence Summaries are contained in F.S. Regs., Part II. and the Staff Manual respectively. Title Pages will be prepared in manuscript.

Place	Date	Hour	Summary of Events and Information	Remarks and references to Appendices
HENEN COURT	Feby 20th		I made out weekly Mollein Returns. G.R.M.	
	21st		I inspected the Animals of the 96th Inf. Brigade. G.R.M.	
	22nd		I had a D.R.O. put in about large numbers of picked up nails. G.R.M.	
	23rd		I inspected the Animals of the 11th H.A.J. & 90th Field Ambulance. G.R.M.	
	24th		I inspected the animals of the 14th Royers Regt, Manchester Regt & Dorset Regt. G.R.M. I made out the G.O.C's advance report on "FLANAGAN". I had a D.R.O. put in about Crops & Sport nails. G.R.M.	
	25th		Office all day. G.R.M.	
	26th		I inspected the Horses in the Reclam of the 14th Reserve Park at ALBERT N.C.O's taking 160 Brigade R.G.A. I gave a lecture on Animal Management at 2.o'clock to the D.A.C & 168th Brigade at BEAUCOURT & at 3 o'clock to the 155th Brigade at MONTIGHMY. A suspicious Cow Disease was reported to me. G.R.M.	
	27th		I made out returns & made a 20 m. on the 2 run with R/E MILLS & ANDERSON AVS. I inspected the horses & mules of the 15th & 17th & J. they looked well. G.R.M.	
	28th		Sent a calf which had died of this mysterious disease to the R.V.C. London. G.R.M.	
	29th		Office all day. G.R.M.	

ADVS 32
DW
Vol 4

WAR DIARY of A.D.V.S. 32nd Div.

INTELLIGENCE SUMMARY

Army Form C. 2118

(Erase heading not required.)

Place	Date	Hour	Summary of Events and Information	Remarks and references to Appendices
HENEN COURT	MARCH 1st		Inspected the horses of the B.A.C. 168th Brig. R.A. & 18th Brig. & B. Battery & B. Battery & B.A.C. 164 Brig. R.F.A. I made a P.M. on a Bull at 3.30 p.m. I attended the G.O.C. conference of Batteries. G.R-m.	
	2nd		Inspected the animals of the B. & D. B.A.C. 155th Brig. & then went and saw several cows down with a most mysterious disease. G.R-m.	
	3rd		Sent off samples of milk to be examined. Went over the D.D.V.S. 4th Army. G.R-m.	
	4th		Office all day. G.R-m.	
	5th		Inspected the sick in B. Bty 164th Brig in mud. Staff. I went to see the horses at 10th Corps H.Q. 2 S.O. at 8 p.m. I went to see some horses of W.A.R. Coy which had died suddenly. G.R-m.	
	6th		D.D.V.S. 4th Army came to see our Johnson Him, the School Camp Bergueneaux. G.R-m.	
	7th		The D.A.D.S. from 10th Corps then the petrol camp. Inspected all the animals in 19 Lane. Two. I went to ALBERT to see the Applicant's horses, 161st Brig. & all the Batteries A.B.C. & D. Batteries 161st Brig. G.R-m.	
	8th		Went all the aft. with M. BIRKIN R.V.C. inspecting A.B.C. & D. Batteries 161st Brig. G.R-m. Spent some time in the Div. Animal Forge. G.R-m.	
	9th		I went to ALBERT completed the horses of A.B. & C. Batteries. In the afternoon I went to see the horses of the Div. Forge & then went to Div. Train on Animal Management. G.R-m.	
	10th		Prepared notes for Units on Animal Management. G.R-m. The 10th Corps at TEUTON COURT. In aft. I went to see the animals of the 96th Inf. Brigade. Inspected all the animals of the 96th Inf. Brigade. In the evening I took the notes on animal management to the Staff Capt. 2 COY R.E. at AVELUY.	
	11th		Spent some time in the Div. Forge. G.R-m.	
	12th		Inspected the horses of X & Y Batteries R.H.A. in morning & the horses 164th Brigade R.F.A. in the afternoon. G.R-m.	
	13th		Inspected the pick of A.B.C. & D. Brig 168th Brig. with Lt. FLANAGAN A.V.C. & then all the horses of the 1/1st London R.G.A. & 1/50 2 A. R.E. & then I went to the station to meet Lt. DOBIE who arrived to replace Lt. FLANAGAN. Lt. D. left that afternoon for the Base. G.R-m. In the afternoon Lt. DOBIE & I went to take some blood from a dying cow.	

WAR DIARY of A.D.V.S. 32nd Div.

or INTELLIGENCE SUMMARY

(Erase heading not required.)

Army Form C. 2118

Place	Date	Hour	Summary of Events and Information	Remarks and references to Appendices
	13/14th		Spent off. Blood & Abbis to R.V.C. & got rd DOB/E A.V.C. to Rt DERT mob. BIRKIN who took DOB/E round to see the Batteries at MOULIN de PIVIER. Spent the p.m. of 14th at DERT mob. the 111th London Brigade. Staff. I went to WARLOY & inspected the M.V.S. & found all in good orders.	
	15th		Went on to see the Train. G.R.m. In aft. the animals of T.M. & C. Batteries 168th Brig. R.F.A. & Bakery Co. I went with Lt DOB/E to inspect the Remount Corrs. G.R-m.	
	16th		D.D.R came to inspect Remount Corrs. G.R.m.	
	17th		I inspected the sick Btty's Bdo 10 Corps G.R.m.	
			Took Blood from a Cow (sent away to be examined) & then inspected the 96th M.G.Co	
	18th		I went to see the animals of the (Army) G.R-m. In aft I again took Blood from Spinal Cord	
			& inspected the animals of the 97th Inf. Brigade. from Cow. G.R.m.	
	19th		Office all day G.R.M.	
	20th		Inspected horses of the D.A.C. & all the D.A.C. & 155th Brig. G.R.m.	
	21st		Spent morning in Sir. Forge.	
	22nd		Spent most of the morning in Sir. Forge. Warped & then inspected 2 Btty 153rd Brig. G.R.m.	
	23rd		Inspected the M.V.S. & visited 2 to be destroyed & then on to the R.G.A. G.R.m.	
			I went to TEUTONCOURT & handed over all the animals of 10 Corps to Capt. M/Laws. In afternoon Inspected	
	24th		a Conference at D.D.R.S. G.R-m. the 14th M. Gun Co. & 14th R. amb & in aft the 96th M.G.C. G.R.m.	
	25th		Inspected the animals 8/14th M.G.Co. & off. all the A.V.C. Sergeants came to see me. G.R-m.	
	26th		Inspected animals Riding R.G.H.Q. & 3rd Bridging Train G.R-m.	
	27th		Inspected the horses of the 111th & 2.36 Co Army Troops. G.R-m.	
	28th		Inspected the M.V.S. Train & advised some to be sent to M.V.S.	
			Took Blood from Cow. Inspected with J.O.C. G.R-m.	
	29th		Attended conference with T.O.C. 15th Brig 168th Brig & D. Bty 164 Brig & 91st Field Amb. G.R.m.	
	30th		Inspected the horses of R.A.C.	
			I examined men all the morning who had undergone a course of instruction at Pin Forge. um aft I	
	31st		inspected with Pt BIRKIN the horses in & B Btys 161st Brig G.R.m.	
			Office all day G.R-m.	

WAR DIARY of F.A.D.V.S. 32nd 2nd Div.
INTELLIGENCE SUMMARY
(Erase heading not required.)

Army Form C. 2118

Instructions regarding War Diaries and Intelligence Summaries are contained in F. S. Regs., Part II. and the Staff Manual respectively. Title Pages will be prepared in manuscript.

Place	Date	Hour	Summary of Events and Information	Remarks and references to Appendices
HENEN COURT	April 1st		Officer on morning & made out Returns. In afternoon went to put about & specially elected Services in 9th Field Ambulance & the sick on X.V. Batteries R.H.A. G.R.M.	
	2nd		Received a grievance through on Sergt. Corpl. A.V.C. G.R.M.	
	3rd		Sturnin moved to SENLIS. G.R.M.	
	4th		Arranged about the 2 forges, & where Hay should be m/s & for making shoes & for horse bearing to shoe. G.R.M.	
	5th		Inspected the forges in the morning & in the afternoon Inspected the animals of the Manchester Regt arranged with the Staff-Captain 14" Infy Brigade about the men in the brigade who had been previously employed on Carel Forges. G.R.M.	
	6th		Inspected 10" Corps H.Q. Div. the animals in the Immortelling Trailers & 16" Northumberland Fusiliers & 17" Field Co R.E. G.R.M.	
	7th		3 more Farriers & 14 men in the Manchester Regt. who had previously been Employed on Carel Forges Inspected & M.V.S & found all in good order owing to the change of billets had to rearrange all the duties of the F.O.P. &c according to orders. Instr. H. BRASSEY A.V.C. VO to the 5" BRIDGING TRAIN which had just arrived up from PLYMOUTH. G.R.M.	
	8th		After all the morning Invent to AMIENS ab.3 & bought 100 Canel Hair Brushes. G.R.M.	
	9th		H. BIRKIN A.V.C. came to see me about taking on for another year & applying for 2 months leave & then to go to the Base for Surgical work. Sent off Returns. G.R.M.	
	10th		Inspected the horses in B & C Batteries 164" Brigade & B & D Batteries 168" Brigade R.F.A. J.R.M.	
	11th		Inspected Batteries in D Battery 168" Brig & Ks 5" Bridging Train & B & C Batteries 164" Brigade R.F.A.	
	12th		Invent round both the Forges Inspected the sick in A & D Batteries 168" & and & the make which had arrived & found members & Saddlemen. J.R.M.	
	13th		Inspected the animals on the 92nd Field Amb. N.B. a C 148" R.F.a. & 19" R.a.c. Fusiliers & had lunch in 96" Infy Brigade & 96" Machine Gun Co & distributed the Remounts. G.R.M.	
	14th		Inspected A B C & D Batteries 155" Brigade R.F.a. started 26 horses with mallein on the 5" Bridging Train. Invent to see the H. A. D.V.S. 8th Div. about some Army troops. G.R.M.	

Army Form C. 2118

WAR DIARY of A.D.V.S. 32nd Div

INTELLIGENCE SUMMARY
II

(Erase heading not required.)

Instructions regarding War Diaries and Intelligence Summaries are contained in F.S. Regs., Part II. and the Staff Manual respectively. Title Pages will be prepared in manuscript.

Place	Date	Hour	Summary of Events and Information	Remarks and references to Appendices
HENEN COURT	APRIL 15th		Interviewed 6 men in 19th Battn. who had previously been employed in Argentin Coal Life but found that they were only strikers. I visited the M.V.S. & it impeded the horses previously tested with mallein & did not find any reactors. J.R.m.	
	16th		I made out Returns all the morning till 11 & then inspected the animals in R.A.C. 155th Brig R.J.a. 218. C.R.E. & 16th Lane Fusiliers & 14th M. Gun C. J.R.m.	
	17th		A.D.V.S. 4th Army came to examine at BIRKIN a R.E. Mule horse & re-engaging & then he inspected the M.V.S. J.R.m.	
	18th		Inspected A & D Batteries 168th Brig. R.F.A., 164th Brig. R.F.A. J.R.m.	
	19th		Inspected A & C Batteries 168th Brig., 1 M. Gun of A.C. I inspected the M.V.S. & found everything in good order. J.R.m.	
	20th		Inspected the animals in the 16th Lane Fusiliers again & a 87th, 168th Brig. again & D Battery 161st Brig. R.F.A. C Battery 168th Brig. & ordered 3 in the D.A.C. to be sent to the M.V.S. J.R.m.	
	21st		Inspected the animals the 15th H.L.I. 2.19 — C.R.E. his afternoon he Third Quarters J 164: 168: Brigade R.F.a. & C Battery 161st Brig. & 14. Reserve Park (1 Section) J.R.m.	
	22nd		Inspected the anon alone in the N.O.Y.L.I., 97th M. Gun Co., 206. C.R.E. & 17th H.L.I. J.R.m. 9 man 2.8 m on open joint cases. J.R.m.	
	23rd 24th		Office all day & spent off examining. J.R.m. Inspected the R.A.C. 18.1st Brig & found everything in very good order in then the R.A.C. 168th Brig R.F.A. ordered to be evacuated for debility. J.R.m. 164th Brigade & the R.A.C. 168th Brig. R.F.A.	
	25th		I took 28 BRASNET his orders to move to Army Head Quarters & then I saw the horses at the M.V.S. which were going to be evacuated & then to see a Debility Command & rating 153rd Brig. in Rear in Div. Train & I walked round the lines of 93rd C Battery 164th Brig. in the Evening. J.R.m.	

WAR DIARY F.A.D.V.S. 32nd Division

INTELLIGENCE SUMMARY

Army Form C. 2118

(Erase heading not required.)

Place	Date	Hour	Summary of Events and Information	Remarks and references to Appendices
	26" 27"			
	28th		Re-examined three S. Smiths & Jan Kerr Certificates. Offices in the aft. 7. a.m. Handed over to Capt J.J. Mills a.r.c. on going on leave. 11.y. a.m.	
	29th		Instructed Lieut. BIRKIN to call & be signed and agreement for Temp. Commission in A.V.C. I forwarded same to D.D.V.S. 4th Army. 11 a.m. Office in the afternoon. Inspected Divisional Forge. 4 p.m.	
	30th		Sent weekly returns to D.D.V.S. 4th army. Office in the afternoon 5 p.m.	

Army Form C. 2118

(Volume 6.)

WAR DIARY
of A.D.V.S. 32nd Div.
INTELLIGENCE SUMMARY
(Erase heading not required.)

Instructions regarding War Diaries and Intelligence Summaries are contained in F. S. Regs., Part II. and the Staff Manual respectively. Title Pages will be prepared in manuscript.

Place	Date	Hour	Summary of Events and Information	Remarks and references to Appendices
SEWZ 15	May 1st		Spent the afternoon at the Office. Completed diary for previous month. J.M.	
	2nd		At the Office in the afternoon. Inspected the Div. Forge 3p.m.	
	3rd		At the Office in the afternoon. I spoke to Capt Mahlo re a supply of linseed oil for their horses of the Artillery.	
	4th		Inspected the Div. Forge. Received a note from O.C. South Irish Horse requesting the return of S.Smith Byrne to his unit (S.I.H.) J.M.	
	5th		At the Office. In the afternoon. Inspected Div. Forge. Shoeing Smith Byrne under instruction at the Div. Forge returned to his unit J.M.	
	6th		At the Office in the afternoon sent J.B. weekly returns J.M. Capt. MILLS a.v.c. came to see me. G.R-m. Inspected the M.V.S. & found all in good order & then the Ironriding Bakery R.G.A. Went to see the D.D.G.S., & Brig. R.F.A. G.R-m. Inspected all the horses in the 155th Brig. R.F.A. in the morning & attended D.D.V.S.	
	7th			
	8th			
	9th		conference at 2-30 & at 6 inspected the horses of the 161st Brigade horses. G.R-m.	
	10th		Inspected the animals about to be evacuated from the M.V.S. & took over from Capt MILLS about to proceed on leave. Inspected the Div. Forge. G.R-m.	
	11th		With the A.D.M.S. Inspected the animals in the 92nd Field Amb. all in good order & the 90th Field Amb. not so good & the shoeing bad. I inspected the Reserve Park & B & C Batteries 164th Brig. G.R-m.	

1875 Wt. W593/826 1,000,000 4/15 J.B.C. & A. A.D.S.S./Forms/C. 2118.

(Volume 6)

Army Form C. 2118

WAR DIARY of A.D.V.S.
INTELLIGENCE SUMMARY 32nd Div.

(Erase heading not required.)

Place	Date	Hour	Summary of Events and Information	Remarks and references to Appendices
SENLIS	12th		Office all the morning with Returnets. In the afternoon Inspected the M.V.S. & the Lancashire Fusiliers. T.R.m.	
	13th		I examined S. Smithson the morning & visited the M.V.S. in the afternoon. I spoke to the A.D.V.S. re getting chains for horses instead of stair-ropes & attended a lecture on dogs. T.R.m.	
	14th		Office all day. T.R.m.	
	15th		I examined S/S Smith's & inspected the M.V.S. & of No. 6 Co. R.A.C. & 161st Brigade R.F.A.	
	16th		Inspected the animals on the Inniskilling Fusiliers, 206 Co R.E. Cable Section (A.C.) T.R.M. MANCHESTERS & D.O.R. SETS. I inspected the M.V.S. & showed the V.O's M.E.O. of B batteries & Inf. Third men of M.V.S. where the advanced collecting station was going to be etc. & in evening Inspected the 15th Lanc. Fusiliers. T.R.m.	
	17th		Inspected the B.A.C. which are shortly to be broken up. Like M.V.S. (& fans out.) & C Battery 161st R.F.A. T.R.m.	
	18th		I went with Staff Captain & saw all the gun limbers & spent the aft. at the M.F.S. T.R.M.	
	19th		Inspected the D.A.C. 155th & H.Q. 25 Co a S.E. & M.V.S. T.R.m.	
	20th		Inspected the B.A.C 161, 168 & 155 T.R.m.	
	21st		Office all day. T.R.M.	
	22nd		Went to see A.D.V.S. 36th Div. re some horses. D.D.R. & D.D.V.S. came by same T.R.m.	
	23rd		Inspected the A.D.V.S. Transport & Dorsets. Both looked very well. In evening I transferred some horses from the R.A. to the infantry. T.R.m.	

Army Form C. 2118
No. 133
(Volume 6)

WAR DIARY
INTELLIGENCE SUMMARY
(Erase heading not required.)

Instructions regarding War Diaries and Intelligence Summaries are contained in F. S. Regs., Part II. and the Staff Manual respectively. Title Pages will be prepared in manuscript.

Place	Date	Hour	Summary of Events and Information	Remarks and references to Appendices
	24th		I distributed the horses from the R.A. to the 8th Corps & 49th Div. The D.D.R. & D.D.V.S. came to see me. J.R-m.	
	25th		I inspected the M.V.S. in the morn & went to see the O.C. 155 "Brig" & in aft 6 P.m. I inspected the horses of the 14th Reserve Park. J.R-m.	
	26th		I went to WARLOY & BELLE EGLISE re the B.A.C. going away. Lot J. Lunch to see how many & smiths the R.A. turn'd had. J.R-m.	
	27th		I inspected 1 section of the B.A.C. I made a P on a mule & to see O.C. 155th Brigade R.J.A. I attended a lecture on LOOS at 3 < J.O.C. conference at 5-30. J.R-m.	
	28th		I attended a lecture in the afternoon with their O.C. the 14th Reserve Park. J.R-m. Office all the morning. I inspected	
	29th		I lectured on Animal Management & gave 4 typewritten copies of notes to D.Battery 161 & C.Batt 168. J.R-m.	
	30th		I attended the Casting by D.D.R. & therejudged in the Competition in C.Battery 168th Brigade. at 6 I gave a lecture to a Battery 164 D.C.Battery 161 Lat 6-45 to B & B Batteries 164 Bde J.R-m.	
	31st		I witnessed funeral O.C. in the mtng re Lectures & grazing. I inspected the M.V.S. I gave Lecture to a Battery 168 "Brig. I inspected their horses which looked well. J.R-m.	

WAR DIARY or INTELLIGENCE SUMMARY

Army Form C. 2118.

A.D.V.S. 32nd Div. Vol 7. June

Place	Date	Hour	Summary of Events and Information	Remarks and references to Appendices
SENLIS	June 1		Inspected the horses of A Battery 164 Brig. R.F.A. & C Battery 161. I went to see the O.C. 155 Brigade. at 5-30 p.m. I gave a lecture on animal management to B & C Batteries 188th Brig. F.O.E.-M.	
	2	10 a.m.	Inspected D. Battery 168 & C Battery 164. D 161 Horses were very bad.	
		2-30	Inspected 49th R.C.A. at 3-30 Inspected round all the 155th Brigade. F.O.-M. Office all the morn. In aft. I gave a lecture to the 49th W. Riding Battery. Inspected the 90" Field Amb. F.O.-M.	
	3			
	4		Inspected No 3 Section D.A.C. & M.V.S. F.O.-M. Went to see the A.D.V.S. 19th Div. F.O.-M. Office in morn. at 3 p.m.	
	5		Inspected No 2 Section D.A.C. & a Bats 161. F.O.-M.	
	6		Inspected the 24, 27, H, 13, 257 Field B.R.E. F.O.-M.	
	7	2 p.m.	I gave a lecture to D 161 & went to arrange about Horse Show. I went in my Flanagan on advanced Vety Collecting Station to B.D.V.S. F.O.-M.	
	8		Inspected the R & A Waggon Lines & gave out notes re Shoeing. F.O.-M. with H. Battery examined 3 S. Smiths. at 6 p.m. & anderson & I inspected the 14.F.B. F.O.-M.	
	9		Inspected all the horses that Parkers. F.O.-M.	
	10		Made arrangements for Horse Show in morning. Horse Show in the afternoon. F.O.-M.	
	11		Inspected the 119 Fd. Co., D 161, B 161, D 164 & C 164. Seal off. F. returns. F.O.-M.	
	12		Inspected the M.V.S. & the H. Batteries in the 49th Division. F.O.-M.	
	13th		At the Office during the afternoon. visited Lieut. Barge. A.D.V.S. on arrival. JJM	
	14th		At the office in the afternoon. Lieut. Smith A.V.C. returns from leave. JJM	
	15th		At office in the afternoon. JJM	
	16th		" " " " " " JJM	
	17th		At the Office in the afternoon. Sent off returns(weekly) to D.D.V.S. JJM	

WAR DIARY or INTELLIGENCE SUMMARY

Army Form C. 2118.

Place	Date	Hour	Summary of Events and Information	Remarks and references to Appendices
SENLIS	18th		At office during the afternoon. Visited A.D.V.S. Office during the afternoon. Spent afternoon at A.D.V.S. Office. A.D.V.S. returned from Leave 5pm	
	19th		Visited A.D.V.S. Office during the afternoon	
	20th		Spent afternoon at A.D.V.S. Office. A.D.V.S. returned from leave 5pm	
	21st		Went over to D.R.S. 36" Div. re travelling. Inspected He'd No 3. G.R.M.	
	22nd		Relieved Capt. & No 3 Batteries 161.	
	23rd		Went round the Gun positions & lines & arranged for Capt Smith to go to Reserve. Inspected He'd Nos 2 and 3. A.O. allotted the duties of the F.O. G.R.M.	
	24th		Inspected operation orders all the morning & at 2 Inspected with Pt. Smith the 10th Brigade. G.R.M.	
	25th		Office in morning & Inspected with Pt. Anderson A.Y.C.H. Forward Maneuver Rgt & 17 Battery. Sub lines & 3 Coys R. Munro Battalion S.W.B at 2½ pm	
	26th		Acting A.T.O.R. a.r.c. to 14th H.A. Group came to see me. G.R.M.	
			V.O. came to see me. Inspected the Engrs 8/13 rs, 3/58.C 56. Workshop & Horses in C15ST, a 168, B164, a 164. Went over O.C. 22,24 & 16 re the Horses Jumping &c.	
			A.D.V.S. G.F. Almy. G.R.M.	
	27th		Inspected with Pt. Anderson the Morris & our & Anderson in the afternoon. Attended G.O.C. Conference at 5-30. G.R.M.	
	28th		Inaine 5 pm on a Strikes died of Ruptured Stomach in 114 H.B. In afternoon Inspected the 91,96th Inf. Brigade rats Inspected the 8 Heavy Batteries. G.R.M.	
	29th		Inspected D1255, C 161, B161 and 2 Horses the 14 Inf. Brigade & army M.T. M.T.S. 76 M.T. duty 1st Battery, & tested 9 Horses A.D.V.S. to see Div. G.R.M.	
	30th		W.O came to see me. Motor out to Rakins.	

32/ July
Army Form C. 2118.
"A D V S
Vol 8

WAR DIARY
or
INTELLIGENCE SUMMARY
(Erase heading not required.)

CONFIDENTIAL

WAR DIARY
OF
A.D.V.S, 32ⁿᵈ DIVISION

VOLUME VIII

From July 1ˢᵗ 1916
to July 31ˢᵗ 1916

Army Form C. 2118.

WAR DIARY A.D.V.S. 32nd Div.

INTELLIGENCE SUMMARY

(Erase heading not required.)

Instructions regarding War Diaries and Intelligence Summaries are contained in F.S. Regs., Part II. and the Staff Manual respectively. Title Pages will be prepared in manuscript.

Place	Date	Hour	Summary of Events and Information	Remarks and references to Appendices
SENLIS	July 1		Inspected the M.V.S. & sent off weekly returns. G.R-m.	
"	2		Inspected the M.V.S. & at night went to see the advanced Collecting station at BOUZEN -COURT. G.R-m.	
"	3		Rode round all the Batteries & all the V.Ops came to see me also the O.C. 25th M.V.S. G.R-m.	
"	4		Inspected the M.R.S. & left for CONTAY & went on my way to see the A.D.V.S. 49 Div. G.R-m.	
CONTAY	5		Inspected the A.D.V.S. 25th Div. & then inspected the M.V.S. at 5-30 & went round the Evacuating & Field Amb. & the Divisional Train. G.R-m.	
"	6		Went to see the D.D.V.S. & showed him my report on the M.V.S. Inspected the Signal Co. & visited the Watering Troughs which were 4 feet deep & saw the Staff Captain R.F.A. & R.G.A. & got fatigues to clean up & cart Chalk about to dry out. G.R-m.	
"	7		Heard we were in Reserve along & went to see the D.D.V.S. & saw the M.V.S. & met Pt. & went to SENLIS & inspected the animals to be evacuated from the M.V.S. at night. G.R-m.	
"	8		HAYTOR at 2H. Bty. R.G.A. & moved to WARLOY. G.R-m.	
WARLOY	9		Inspected all the animals in the D.A.C. G.R-m.	
"	10		Went to BOUZINCOURT & spent the morning at SENLIS getting the ground round the water troughs repaired. G.R-m.	
"	11		Inspected the Water Troughs all day. Inspected the M.V.S. G.R-m.	
"	12		Dined at the Town Major & R.G.A. G.R-m.	
"	13		Inspected the M.V.S. also 119 & 49 R.G.A. & also pone animals in the D.A.C. Inspected with Col. HAYTOR A.V.C. the 49 R.G.A. G.R-m.	
"			Inspected with Col. HAYTOR A.V.C. the 114" & moved to BOUZENCOURT at night. G.R-m.	
BOUZEN COURT	14		Inspected animals & evacuated in the M.V.S. & then went to Col. HAYTOR about water troughs. G.R-m. I asked the Town Major to see about the Transport Officer re 2 men getting hay R.G.A. I paid the Transport Officer.	
"	15		Inspected the horses in 17th L.S. & paw the A.D.V.S. 25th Division to a conference at a D.S. as S. Smiths. Inspected with A.D.V.S. 25th Division to a Conference at a D.S. G.R-m.	

WAR DIARY or INTELLIGENCE SUMMARY

(Erase heading not required.)

Army Form C. 2118

A.D.V.S. 32nd Division

Place	Date	Hour	Summary of Events and Information	Remarks and references to Appendices
BOUZIN COURT	July 16		I left at 10 a.m. & spent all the morning with the R.G.A. I rode to BEAUVAL in the afternoon & went round the R.G.A. Brigs. to BEAUVAL.	
BEAUVAL	17		I took report of casualties to D.D.V.S. G.H.Q. I left for DOULLENS the last 14 days to G.O.C. & D.D.M.S.	
DOULLENS	18		Left for DOULLENS. G.R-m.	
"	19		Inspected the M.V.S. & G.R-m about procedure on leaving horses behind. France. Regt. for FLERS G.R-m.	
FLERS	20		I saw the Staff Captain R.A.	
BRYAS	21		Rode to BRYAS G. LILLERS G.R-m. I went round a French Vety. Hospital on the way.	
			Left at 9 & arrived at DOULLENS at 1. G.R-m.	
		4.30 p.m.	I went to see the 17th H.J. G.R-m.	
LILLERS	22	10 a.m.	I went with Capt ANDERSON A.V.C. to see the 162nd L.J. at 2.15 p.m. to 2 D.V.S. & D.D.R.	
			came to see me & went to see the Head Qrs. Company Div. Train. G.R-m.	
"	23rd	10-30	Inspected the Horses of the 161st Brig. R.J.A. and 3rd M.H.16 2nd Brigade at 2 a. G.R-m.	
"	24th		Inspected the 1st Brigade R.J.A. in afternoon the M.V.S. G.R-m.	
"	25th	9.30	D.D.V.S. & D.D.R. inspected the animals in 155 & 161 L.D.A.C. G.R-m.	
		3 p.m.	Went to see horses magot or invalided by Major PALLIN & rode G.R-m.	
			Inspected the 168th Bay R.J.A. & rode to BETHUNE G.R-m.	
"	26th	10 a.m.	D.D.V.S. came where the M.V.S. was to god met the A.D.V.S. 8th Div. Inspected the	
BETHUNE	27	10 am	I went to see the Signal Co. G.R-m.	
			animals in the 168th Brigade those stores. G.R-m. in the afternoon. G.R-m	
"	28th		I judged at the 168th Brigade those stores. G.R-m	
"	29th		On Office all day. I went out to see No 1/c D.A.C. in the afternoon. G.R-m.	
"	30th		D.D.V.S. came to see me G.R-m.	
"	31st		Inspected the 1st m. Gun Co. 1st DORSETS & 2nd 6th ROYAL SCOTS. G.R-m.	
		5.30	Had a Conference of F.O.O. G.R-m	

Army Form C. 2118.

WAR DIARY
or
INTELLIGENCE SUMMARY
(Erase heading not required.)

Vol 2

Confidential

War Diary Vol. II
of
A.D.V.S. 32nd Divn.

From Aug. 1st to Aug. 31st /16.

Vol IX

WAR DIARY
INTELLIGENCE SUMMARY
A.D.V.S. 32nd Div.

Army Form C. 2118.

(Erase heading not required.)

Place	Date	Hour	Summary of Events and Information	Remarks and references to Appendices
BETHUNE	Aug 1		Inspected the 97th Inf. Brigade & sent Diary. J.R-m.	
	2	10 a.m	Inspected the Inniskilling Fusiliers, 16th N. Bttn & 96th Machine Gun Company. J. Morris.	
		6 p.m	Gave a lecture to the R.E. on Animal Management. J. R-m.	
	3	9 a.m	Saw animals evacuated by the Barge & inspected the 15th & 16th Lancashire Fusiliers. J. R-m.	
	4	9 a.m	Inspected the M.V.S. & at 6 p.m. I gave a lecture to the 97th Machine Gun Company. J.R-m.	
	5	8-30 a.m	Saw horses put on Barge & inspected horses on the Signal Company & had a General Ambulance horse tested with Mallein. J. R-m.	
	6		Attended A.D.V.S. Conference. J. R-m.	
	7		Inspected the R.O.Y.L. J & Head Quarters, 63rd C Batteries 160th Brig at the standings of A.B. D.O. Batteries 161st Brig. J. R-m.	
	8		Inspected A & B Batteries 164th & 15th H.A.G. & the standings of B & C 155th J. R-m.	
	9		Spent the day at the Vety Hospitals at ABBEVILLE. J.R-m.	
	10		Inspected the wounded horses in R.A. at Sir. Tram & attended C.O.s Conference. J. R-m.	
	11		Inspected animals to be evacuated at C 155th J. R-m.	
	12		Attended Castings by A.D.S. & inspected the A Battery 164th Brigade. J. R-m.	
	13		Office all day. J. R-m.	
	14		Inspected the D.A.C. & the Red Star Pits. J. R-m.	
	15	8 a.m	Inspected animals to be evacuated at A & B 161 & at 2 p.m. Inspected H.Q. & 164 Brig & 2 Machine Gun Company & C 161. J. R-m.	
	16	10 a.m	Inspected A 160 & B 155. At 4 p.m. I went with the G.O.C. round all the Battery Wagon lines & arranged about the standings. J.R-m.	
	17	8 a.m	I met the Remounts at Station at 8 a.m. on to M.V.S. & inspected the 90th Field Ambulance & at 2 p.m. the 96th Field Ambulance. J. R-m.	
	18		Office in morning. At 2 I went round all the Infantry Transport with the G.O.C. J. R-m. With Capt Anderson V.O. 1/2 Corps A.S.C. J. R-m.	
	19		I went round the Infantry Units & M & 3 Corp A.S.C. J. R-m.	

WAR DIARY A.D.V.S. 32nd Div.

or

INTELLIGENCE SUMMARY

(Erase heading not required.)

Army Form C. 2118.

Place	Date	Hour	Summary of Events and Information	Remarks and references to Appendices
BETHUNE	20		Office all day. J. R-m.	
	21		Went to try & investigate the outbreak of Colic in the 168th Brigade.	
		2-pm	Gave a lecture at the Div. School. J. R-m.	
	22		Saw horses evacuated on Barges when went to see about the Water Troughs & Standing in & C 168 & attended a P.M. & saw all the A.V.C. Sergeants Wallets. J. R-m.	
	23		Inspected the 11th Border Regt & the Phoenix J. No 2 & 3 Co A.S.C. J. R-m.	
	24		K. Orr came to see me. J. R-m.	
	25		D.D.V.S. inspected the M.V.S. & 168th N. Mid. R.F.A. & A 161. at 2. He inspected the 96th Inf. Brigade & 164 Brigade R.F.A. J. R-m.	
	26		Went with Capt MILLS to find a suitable place for an advanced Collecting Station & then to see the Standings for Horses in 14th Inf. Brigade. J. R-m.	
	27		Office all day. J. R-m.	
	28		Capt. G.M. RICHARDSON A.V.C. arrived & Capt. BIRKIN A.V.C. left. I went round with the above 2 Officers the 155 & 161 Brigades R.F.A. J. R-m.	
	29		Inspected the 15th & the 97th Inf. Brigade at 17th N.F. J. R-m.	
	30		Inspected horses for carting in the Inf. Brigades. At 2p.m. I went to see the M.V.S. & horses of Siv. J. 2 Div. J. R-m. I visited the 90th Field Ambulance. J. R-m.	
	31		D.V.S & D.D.V.S. inspected the M.V.S. & at 2.p.m. the 90th Field Ambulance. J. R-m.	

Army Form C. 2118

Vol. 10

WAR DIARY
or
INTELLIGENCE SUMMARY
(Erase heading not required.)

Confidential
War Diary
of
A.D.V.S. 32nd Divn.
from Sept 1st to Sept 30th 1916

Vol. X.

WAR DIARY

Vol. X — A.D.V.S. 32nd Div.

INTELLIGENCE SUMMARY

Army Form C. 2118.

Place	Date	Hour	Summary of Events and Information	Remarks and references to Appendices
BETHUNE	Sept 1st		Office in morn. In aft. I inspected some Inf. Units. J. R-m.	
	2nd		I inspected the horses in A 155 & D 161. J. R-m.	
	3rd		All V.Os came to see me at 11 & at 3 I attended a conference at D.D.V.S. J. R-m.	
	4th		I gave wastage returns to Staff Captains. J. R-m.	
	5th		I inspected the 92nd Field Ambulance in the afternoon. J. R-m.	
	6th		Office all the morn. I inspected the R.E. in the afternoon. J. R-m.	
	7th		I inspected the 96th Inf. Brigade in the morning & the Staff Captains re various matters. J. R-m.	
	8th		I inspected the 17th N.Z. & saw all the S.B Co Sup. Train. J. R-m.	
	9th		I inspected the pick up & Hd. Qr. B. Co Sup. Train. J. R-m.	
	10th		I inspected the morn. In afternoon I took the A.D.E. to the M.V.S. to see about the timber for Stables. I inspected animals to be evacuated. J. R-m.	
	11th		Office in morning & made a P.M. in the afternoon. J. R-m.	
	12th		Office in morning & made a P.M. in the B.A.C. J. R-m.	
	13th		I inspected the pick in the B.A.C. J. R-m.	
			I destroyed 38 Remounts & then inspected the M.V.S. 155 & 161 Brigades R.J.A.	
		2 p.m	I inspected the standings of the 14th Inf. Brigade. J. R-m.	
	14th		I inspected the 164th Brigade. J. R-m.	
	15th		I inspected a 155 & D 155. In aft. inspected the M.V.S. J. R-m.	
	16th		I went to see Capt. DORIE & RICHARDSON a.v.c. & arranged for transfer of cured animals to go to 14th Inf. Brigade. J. R-m.	
	17th		Office all the morn. J. R-m.	
	18th		Office all day. J. R-m.	
	19th		D.D.V.S. inspected animals for casting. I spent the aft. at the M.V.S. J. R-m.	
	20th		I spent the morning at the M.V.S. & in aft. I inspected 18 H.D. to be transferred from the train. J. R-m.	
	21st		I went to M.V.S. J. R-m.	

Army Form C. 2118.

WAR DIARY — **A.D.V.S.**
INTELLIGENCE SUMMARY 32nd Div.

No 823
1.10.16.

(Erase heading not required.)

Instructions regarding War Diaries and Intelligence Summaries are contained in F. S. Regs., Part II. and the Staff Manual respectively. Title Pages will be prepared in manuscript.

Place	Date	Hour	Summary of Events and Information	Remarks and references to Appendices
BETHUNE	Sept 22		Inspected the M.V.S. & some R.A. & Inf. units. J.R-m.	
	23.		I inspected the forge where 2 men are under instruction, & inspected some R.A. & infantry units. J.R-m.	
	24.		I distributed the Remounts & inspected the M.V.S. J.R-m.	
	25		I inspected some animals at the M.V.S. & some Inf. units. J.R-m.	
	26		Inspected some R.E. & Inf. units. J.R-m.	
	27		I went round some R.A. & R.A.S.C. units. J.R-m.	
	28		I went to see Capt. RICHARDSON of 30 B.I.F. & inspected the M.V.S. J.R-m.	
	29.		Office all the morning & I supt. spent the aft. at the M.V.S. superintending the building of the new Stables. J.R-m.	
	30		I inspected the Signal Company & 97th M.Gun Co. & saw the building of Stables at M.V.S. in aft. J.R-m.	

Army Form C. 2118.

WAR DIARY
or
INTELLIGENCE SUMMARY

A.D.V.S. —
32ⁿᵈ Divⁿ

Vol II

Instructions regarding War Diaries and Intelligence Summaries are contained in F.S. Regs., Part II. and the Staff Manual respectively. Title Pages will be prepared in manuscript.

(Erase heading not required.)

Place	Date	Hour	Summary of Events and Information	Remarks and references to Appendices
BETHUNE	Oct 1		Office all day. J.R-m.	
"	2		Inspected the M.V.S. & saw the Remounts distributed & arranged the purchase of some anvils. J.R.m.	
"	3		Inspected on the firing in Stewart's Clipping Machine. J.R-m.	
"	4		Inspected the M.F.S. & 2nd R.F.A. MILLS A.V.C. destroying orders. Saw Capt Mills afterⁿ J.R-m.	
"	5		Inspected the D.D.V.S. the C.R.A. Units. J.R-m.	
"	6		Inquired from Inf. & R.A. the recommendations & implored some Inf. Units. J.R-m.	
"	7		Sent to see D.V.S. re recommendation & inspected all the horse standings 10-1 & 2-6. J.R-m.	
"	8		Conversed the G.O.C. & his inspection of the stabling. J.R-m.	
"	9		Sent round many units to the stabling. J.R-m.	
"	10		Saw round from ENGLAND & attended a lecture on how to use the Stewart's Clipper & adjusting. C.O's carried with Capt RICHARDSON A.V.C. to see the new Battery. J.R-m.	
"	11		Capt PLATT ROBSON, MILLS, DOBIE & J tested with mallein & 15 J.R-m.	
"	12		Re amount of C 155 & inspected the M.V.S. & men under instruction in Div. Forge. about 6 J.R.m. J	
"	13		Attended the GOCA conference & J inspected & arranged to see D.V.S. J.R-m.	
"	14		Recommend J.C. 155 2 Div. visited the different horse standing. J.R-m.	
"	15		Sent the A.D.V.S. 1ˢᵗ army round the different horse standings. J.R-m.	
"	16		Took the D.D.V.S. 2ⁿᵈ Div. & took to J.R-m	
CHAMBERS	17		Handed over to A.D.V.S. 2ⁿᵈ Div & rode to J.R-m.	
LECROY	18		J rode to J.R-m.	
BEAUVAL	19		Beauval moved to J.R-m.	
"	20		Office all day. J.R-m.	
"	21		Office all day. J.R-m.	
			Writing forafstroke with mallein. J.R-m.	
			Saw J. Sutherland with mallein. J.R-m.	
CONTAY	22		To lee adm Division. moved to CONTAY. J went to see D.D. V.S. Reserve army. J.R-m.	
"	23		Office all day. J.R-m.	
			Inspected some of the R.A. & moved to J.R-m.	
BOUZIN COURT	24		J inspected the 97 Inf. Bring. J.R-m.	
"	25		Went to buy 5 Chaff Cutters. J.R.m.	

Army Form C. 2118.

WAR DIARY
or
INTELLIGENCE SUMMARY

A.D.V.S.
32 W Div.

(Erase heading not required.)

Instructions regarding War Diaries and Intelligence Summaries are contained in F. S. Regs., Part II. and the Staff Manual respectively. Title Pages will be prepared in manuscript.

Place	Date	Hour	Summary of Events and Information	Remarks and references to Appendices
	26"		Transferred to M.V.S. J. R-m.	
	27"		Busy re the clipping. J. R-m.	
	28"		Inspected the 97" Inf. Brig. M.L. Bro. D.D.V.S. came to see me. J. R-m.	
	29"		Busy re clipping. J. R-m.	
	30"		Ditto. J. R-m.	
	31"		Ditto. J. R-m.	

Army Form C. 2118.

WAR DIARY of A.D.V.S.
INTELLIGENCE SUMMARY 32nd Div.

Vol. XII

(Erase heading not required.)

Instructions regarding War Diaries and Intelligence Summaries are contained in F.S. Regs., Part II. and the Staff Manual respectively. Title Pages will be prepared in manuscript.

Place	Date	Hour	Summary of Events and Information	Remarks and references to Appendices
BOUZIN COURT	1.		I inspected the 96th & 97th Inf. Brigades. J.R-m.	
	2.		I inspected the M.V.S. D.D.V.S. came to see me. J.R-m.	
	3.		I inspected M.V.S. & 91st Field Ambulance. J.R-m.	
	4.		D.V.S. came to see me & I inspected 90 & 92 Field Ambulance. J.R-m.	
	5.		I inspected animals to be evacuated. J.R-m.	
	6.		I inspected animals to be evacuated. I inspected the 96th Inf. Brig. J.R-m.	
	7.		D.V.S. came to see me & I went to the Railhead. J.R-m.	
	8.		I inspected the horses in Nos 2, 3, & 4 Co A.S.C. & 90th Field Aml. J.R-m.	
	9.		I inspected the M.V.S. J.R-m.	
	10.		I went to AMIENS to arrange about the purchase of Staff Chargers. J.R-m.	
	11.		I inspected the animals to be evacuated. J.R-m.	
	12.		Office all day. J.R-m.	
	13.		I inspected horses to be evacuated & attended G.O.C's conference. J.R-m.	
	14.		Nothing to report. J.R-m.	
	15.		Ready to move. The order was cancelled. J.R-m.	
	16.		I inspected the M.V.S. Major & went to see the A.D.V.S. 2 Wgn. J.R-m.	
	17.		I inspected horses for evacuation. I left for 2 DCo A.S.C. J.R-m.	
BERTRAN COURT	18.		I inspected the 81 Bgde. ammunition & inspected H 2 27 Co A.S.C. J.R-m.	
	19.		I inspected horses of the R.A. Wagon Lines. J.R-m.	
	20.		I inspected the M.V.S. of 155 "Brig". J.R-m.	
	21.		I inspected C Battery 155 "Brig". J.R-m.	
	22.		I went over to the D.A.C. & then to meet the V.O. J.R-m.	
	23.		A.D.V.S. 7th Assn. came to see me. J.R-m.	

Army Form C. 2118.

WAR DIARY
INTELLIGENCE SUMMARY

A.D.V.S.
32nd Divn.

(Erase heading not required.)

Place	Date	Hour	Summary of Events and Information	Remarks and references to Appendices
DOULLENS CANAPLES	24		I went to see V.O.n. J.R-m.	
	25		Started at 10 & went to see Capt. DOBIE A.V.C. & the D.D.V.S. & arrived J.R-m.	
	26		Drove to CANAPLES. J.R-m.	
	27		I went to ST OUEN. J.R-m.	
	28		I inspected Int Units. J.R-m.	
	29		Took over from A.D.V.S. JJM.	
	30th		at A.D.V.S. Office in the morning. Mobile Section moved to ST. OUEN. JJM.	

Army Form C. 2118.

WAR DIARY
or
INTELLIGENCE SUMMARY

(Erase heading not required.)

Confidential
War Diary
of
A.D.V.S. 32nd Div.
from 1st Dec 1916 to 31st Dec 16.

Vol. XII.

WAR DIARY

Vol XII. INTELLIGENCE SUMMARY of A.D.V.S. 39nd Division

Army Form C. 2118.

Place	Date	Hour	Summary of Events and Information	Remarks and references to Appendices
CANAPLES	1st		At the A.D.V.S. Office. 9pm.	
"	2nd		Inspected horses of 21st RESERVE PARK & PRISONERS OF WAR. CAMPS 9pm	
"	3rd		" " " " " of DIV. H.Q. at A.D.V.S Office 9pm.	
"	4th		Inspected 47th. RESERVE. PK. 9pm	
"	5th		At Office in the morning. Inspected French horses with Mange 9pm.	
"	6th		" " " " " morning 9pm	
"	7th		Made enquiries re. CAPT. DOBEY. at 168 BDE. Arranged for CAPT. REED	
			to take Veterinary charge of D.W. AMM. COL. 9pm.	
"	8th		Inspected sick at DIV. H.Q. at Office in the morning 9pm	
"	9th		Cut French dairy at CAMAPLES out of bounds for horses 9pm	
"	10th		At the Office during the morning. 9pm.	

Army Form C. 2118.

WAR DIARY or INTELLIGENCE SUMMARY

(Erase heading not required.)

Place	Date	Hour	Summary of Events and Information	Remarks and references to Appendices
CANAPLES	Dec 11th		Office all day. Inspected the French Cavalry Horses with Mange. J.R-m.	
	12th		V.O. came to see me. J.R-m.	
	13th		Walked to G.O.C. & attended to the Mange Cases. J.R-m.	
	14th		3.D.V.S. came & saw the mange cases. Inspected the M.V.S. J.R-m.	
	15th		Came to AMIENS to buy Linseed & another parcel of Chaff Cutter. J.R-m.	
	16th	10.30	Inspected 13,161 at 2 am. As H6th Rerm Park. J.R-m	
	17th		Office all day. J.R-m.	
	18th		Office all day. J.R-m.	
	19th		Inspected Horses CT.D 168 - Brig R.J.A. Rogers off with the Mange Cases. J.R-m.	
	20th		Inspected C.T.D 161. D. off. I know Prew Ch/S Cutter At AMIENS. J.R-m.	
	21st		I gave the G.O.C. 3.D.V.S. came over to see the Mange Cases. J.R-m.	
	22nd		Inspected C.I.T. & the M.V.S. J.R-m.	
	23rd		All day with the Mange Cases & pariage Rebates. J.R-m.	
	24th		All day with the Mange Cases. J.R-m.	
	25th		Office. J.R-m.	
	26th		Inspected B.C.I.S J.R-m.	
	27th		Office & attended the Mange Cases. J.R-m.	
	28th		Came to TALMAS to give about the disinfection of the Stables with the Manu. I have Brought. Inspected the 46th Resm Park. Just the 3.D.V.S. at the P.V.S. J.R-m.	
	29th		Capt ANDERSON A.V.C. & I inspected the 97th & Inft. Bde Jefferies DDVS. performed inspected WM.G. A.S.C. at 5.30 9am & leave in Animal Management on PUCHVILLERS & 6.30 at RUPEMBRE J.R-m	
	30th		Office, no motor. & Jointstaked the 140 Remounts to swing. J.R-m.	
	31st		3.D.V.S. came & we inspected the 46th Resm Park. J.R-m.	

Army Form C. 2118.

WAR DIARY
or
INTELLIGENCE SUMMARY

(Erase heading not required.)

Vol 14

Confidential

War Diary

of

A. D. V. S. 32nd Division

from 1st of January to 31st January 1917

Vol. No. 14.

Army Form C. 2118.

WAR DIARY
or
INTELLIGENCE SUMMARY

(Erase heading not required.)

J.A.D.V.S. 32nd Div.

Instructions regarding War Diaries and Intelligence Summaries are contained in F.S. Regs., Part II. and the Staff Manual respectively. Title Pages will be prepared in manuscript.

Place	Date	Hour	Summary of Events and Information	Remarks and references to Appendices
CANAPLES	Jany 1917 2		Inspected the 168 Brig in M.V.S. T.R-m.	
	3		Issued orders re Remount management to 96 14th Inf. Brig. T.R-m.	
			Inspected DOULLENS Artillery remount depôt for Reg. Chief Buses. T.R-m.	
			Gave lectures at 5.30 to 96th Inf. Brig. & at 6.30 to 14th Inf. Brig on Remount work.	
	4		Went to PUCHEVILLES to inspect the 3 Suspected Mange cases & as M.O. + Vet.O.	
			& 96th Inf Brig. T.R-m.	
	5		Inspected all pack transport. T.R-m.	
MARIEUX	6		Left for MARIEUX T.R-m.	
	7		Office work. T.R-m	
			New Address T.R-m	
BUS	8		Left for BUS. Inspected M.V.S. T.R-m	
	9		Inspected M.V.S. & went to AMIENS to bring Vet.O. Steven. T.R-m.	
	10		Went round the Inf. Brigades. T.R-m.	
	11		Inspected the new sick lines & 160th Brig. R.S.A. T.R-m	
	12		Inspected M.V.S. & gave a chart & hints to the Travelling Sanitars. T.R-m.	
	13		Inspected M.V.S. T.R-m.	
	14		Inspected M.V.S. & passed 2 m on 3 sick horses. Inspected 90th Field Amb. T.R-m	
	15		Staff Inspected the Inf. Units. T.R-m.	
	16		Inspected shoeing R.A. & Brig. T.R-m.	
	17		Inspected M.V.S. & 90th Field Amb. T.R-m.	
	18		Nothing out in V.S. all day. T.R-m.	
	19		Went to ACHEUX on met Remounts. T.R-m.	
	20		Inspected Signals & M.V.S. in afternoon the 161 & 168 Brig. R.S.A. Hd.	
	21		Sent off Returns. T.R-m.	

Army Form C. 2118.

WAR DIARY
INTELLIGENCE SUMMARY

A.D.V.S.
32nd Div.

(Erase heading not required.)

Place	Date	Hour	Summary of Events and Information	Remarks and references to Appendices
	22		Inspected M.V.S. & went to see O.C. 7th Div. M.V.S. G.R-m.	
	23		Left for BERTRANCOURT. Inspected 83, 161 & the horses to be evacuated from M.V.S. G.R-m.	
BERTRANCOURT	24		Inspected the 155th Tps R.F.A. G.R-m.	
	25		Inspected the 90th Field Amb. 46th Reserve Park, & 21st Reserve Park. G.R-m.	
	26		Inspected 161 & 168 Brigades. G.R-m.	
	27		Went round the 96th Inf. Brigade. G.R-m.	
	28		Inspected M.V.S. G.R-m.	
	29		Went with the A.A. & Q.M.G. round the 161 & 96th Inf. Brigades. G.R-m.	
	30		Went round the 97th Inf. Brigade & the R.E. In aft. inspected the M.V.S. G.R-m.	
	31		Went round the 14th Inf. Bde. Horse & R-m.	

D.A.G.
　3rd Echelon

　　Herewith War Diary of A.D.V.S. for Month of February.
It is regretted that this was omitted from the War Diaries forwarded you on 10/3/17.

　　　　　A.H. Tall (?)
　　　　　Captain
　　　for Brig General
　　　Comdg 32nd Division

15/3/17

WAR DIARY
or
INTELLIGENCE SUMMARY

Army Form C. 2118.

Vol 15

Confidential
War Diary
A.D.V.S. 32nd Div.
from 1st Feb' 17 to 28th Sept 1917
Vol. XV

Army Form C. 2118.

WAR DIARY

A.D.V.S.
32nd Div.

INTELLIGENCE SUMMARY

Vol. XV

(Erase heading not required.)

Place	Date	Hour	Summary of Events and Information	Remarks and references to Appendices
BERTRY COURT	Feby 1		I inspected the horses of 15th Brig. R.F.A. J.R-m.	
	2		I instructed horse of R.A. Inf. J.R-m.	
	3		I attended D.D.V.S. with recent sick cases. J.R-m.	
	4		I inspected M.V.S. J.R-m.	
	5		I inspected M.V.S. & R. Batters 161. Staff. I gave a lecture to R.E. 62nd Div. I inspected after went to see D.D.V.S. J.R-m.	
	6		D.D.V.S. came over to see the Mange Cases in R. 184. I went to see 153 = 8 Batt R.F.A. in aft. J.R-m.	
	7		I inspected the morning with B. 161. J.R-m.	
	8		I spent the morning with B. 161. at 3 p.m. I attended conference at D.D.V.S. J.R-m.	
	9		I spent the morning with B. 161. J.R-m.	
	10		I inspected M.V.S. & B06 & 218" Co R.E. Head Quarters 161 signing 28. 169. Capt. J.m. RICHARDSON A.V.C was discharged from Hospital. J.R-m.	
	11		I inspected the D.A.C. J.R-m.	
	12		I inspected animals for Evacuation & Horses of 90" Field Amb. B. & Battery 161. at 2 p.m. I distributed horses various units. J.R-m.	
	13		I inspected M.V.S. & went to see A.D.V.S. 62nd Div. I inspected B. 161. J.R-m.	
	14		In aft. I took horses passing Chaff Cutters to AMIENS. J.R-m. I inspected B. 161. 155 = B Mg R.F.A.	
	15		I gave orders to Capt SHARPE A.V.C to stay behind with 155 = B Mg R.F.A. (Army artillery now). I transferred some heavy artillery horses to the Div. Tram & I inspected M.V.S. J.R-m.	
	16		I inspected the A.D.V.S. & No.O.C.M.V.S. of the 62nd Div. J.R-m.	
	17		Left at 10 a.m. for VILLERS BOCAGE. J.R-m.	

Army Form C. 2118

WAR DIARY
or
INTELLIGENCE SUMMARY
(Erase heading not required.)

Vol XV (con)

Instructions regarding War Diaries and Intelligence Summaries are contained in F. S. Regs., Part II and the Staff Manual respectively. Title Pages will be prepared in manuscript.

Place	Date	Hour	Summary of Events and Information	Remarks and references to Appendices
VILLERS BOCAGE	July 18th		Inspected M.V.S. J.R-m.	
	19th		Arranged interview with D.D.M.S. 4th Army. J.R-m.	
	20th		Went to see D.D.M.S. 4th Army. J.R-m.	
	21st		Left at 9 a.m. for VILLERS BOCAGE. Inspected the stables of R.a. with Staff Captain to find a suitable place for M.V.S. J.R-m.	
	22nd		Went to see the V.O. of the French Artillery. J.R-m.	
	23rd		Inspected the new lines. J.R-m.	
	24th		Inspected M.V.B. and went to AMIENS to pass a horse	
			and went round R.a. lines.	
			Left here by the R.a. J.R-m.	
	25th		Went round the new wagon lines. J.R-m.	
	26th		Found Vetlet a Stabler for 2 Batteries J.R-m.	
	27th		Inspected the horses of Inf. Units & 91st Field Amb. In aft. Inspected the horses of the range stabling French Field Amb. Type & stables, the horses of 90th Field Amb. and went to the French V.O.	
	28th		In Standard Conference at D.D.V.S. R-m. at S.O.C. mewed D.D.V.O. that all amb. was stabled.	

Army Form C. 2118

WAR DIARY
or
INTELLIGENCE SUMMARY

(Erase heading not required.)

Confidential War Diary of

A.D.M.S. 32nd Division

from

1st March to 31st March 1917

Vol. XVI

Army Form C. 2118

WAR DIARY
of
INTELLIGENCE SUMMARY

D.A.D.V.S. 32nd Div.

Vol. XVI

(Erase heading not required.)

Instructions regarding War Diaries and Intelligence Summaries are contained in F.S. Regs., Part II. and the Staff Manual respectively. Title Pages will be prepared in manuscript.

Place	Date	Hour	Summary of Events and Information	Remarks and references to Appendices
QUESNEL	MARCH 1		I inspected R.E. units. J.R-m.	
	2.		I arranged about the clipping of R.A. horses. In aft. I inspected some of the D.A.C. J.R-m.	
	3		I inspected the horses of Signals & some of the Train. J.R-m.	
	4		I inspected horses being clipped. J.R-m.	
	5.		I inspected horses being clipped. J.R-m.	
	6.		I inspected M.T.S. & some Inf. & R.E. units & 91st Field Ambulance. J.R-m.	
	7.		I inspected the clipping in D.A.C. & Div. Train. J.R-m.	
	8.		Office all day. J.R-m.	
	9.		I inspected some of R.A. horses. J.R-m.	
	10.		I was in office most of the day. J.R-m.	
	11.		I inspected the 90th Field Amb & some of the D.A.C. J.R-m.	
	12.		V.S. came to see me. I inspected H.Qr & Train & M.V.S. J.R-m.	
	13.		I inspected the R.A. Wagon lines & the horses of Divnl. Coys. J.R-m.	
	14.		I inspected horses of 5/6 ROYAL SCOTS. With new C.O. I saw many Inf. Units, several other units. J.R-m.	
	15.		A.D.V.S. 4th Army spent the day & inspected all the R.A. horses & several other Units. J.R-m.	
	16.		I inspected with their V.O. many Inf. Units. J.R-m.	
	17		I inspected the 96th Inf. Brig. Animals in morn & some of the D.A.C. & Div. Train in the afternoon. J.R-m.	

Army Form C. 2118.

WAR DIARY
of
INTELLIGENCE SUMMARY

(Erase heading not required.)

Vol. XVI A.D.V.S. 32nd Divn.

Place	Date	Hour	Summary of Events and Information	Remarks and references to Appendices
QUESNEL WARVIL LERS	18		Inspected Wagon Lines. D.H.Q. moved to 3.R.m.	
	19		I went round the Wagon Lines at QUESNEL & then went to see some of the R.A. Units at ETHUON.	
LEAYWURT	20		M.V.S. Units to LEAYNCOURT. D.H.Q moved to 3.R.m	
NESLE	21		I went round the horses of 168 Field amb some of the 161 & 162 unit of R.A.M.C D.H.Q to NESLE. 3.10-m	
	22		I returned to QUESNEL in main ran a/c inspect some of the R.A. horses 3 R-m	
	23		Capt ANDERSON R.A.C. went to line at YOYEMME & RALLREED A.V.C and H.Q L.R-m	
	24		Inspected some horses in 161 Field Amb 3.R.m.	
	25		I went up to M.Inf. Brig & 95/96 & 159 Inf Brig. R.S.R. J took massage Return to a.a.& Q.M.G. 3. R-m	
	26		Inspected Horses at 96 Inf. Units. 3. R-m.	
	27		Capt Reed G.V.C took in a.D.V.S. proceeded in learn. D.V.R.	
	28		Wrote various units for Divis Artillery details etc D.V.R.	
	29		Divn from NESLE to AURIOR D.V.R	
AURIOR	30		Visited this div & toyrule etc. Visited 14 Inf Bde Otty Br.V.S. D.V.R. enemy death J. I having visited tow down.	
	31		Went round various units & attended Office work D.V.R	

Army Form C. 2118.

WAR DIARY
or
INTELLIGENCE SUMMARY.
(Erase heading not required.)

Instructions regarding War Diaries and Intelligence Summaries are contained in F. S. Regs., Part II. and the Staff Manual respectively. Title pages will be prepared in manuscript.

Confidential

War diary of
A.D.V.S. 32nd Division
from April 1st to April 30th 1917

(Vol XVII)

WAR DIARY
~~INTELLIGENCE SUMMARY~~

(Erase heading not required.)

Army Form C. 2118

Vol. XVII A.D.V.S. 32nd Div.

Instructions regarding War Diaries and Intelligence Summaries are contained in F.S. Regs., Part II. and the Staff Manual respectively. Title Pages will be prepared in manuscript.

Place	Date	Hour	Summary of Events and Information	Remarks and references to Appendices
AUROIR	APRIL 1		Visited my units & attended office	
	2		Visited my units & attended office	Dnr.
	3		Visited my units & attended office	Dnr.
	4		Visited my units & attended office	D.N.R
	5		Visited my units & attended office	Dnr.
	6		Visited my units & attended office	Dnr.
	7		Visited my units & attended office	Dnr.
	8		Visited my units & attended office	Dnr.
	9		Inspected the horses of 168th Brig. R.F.A. with Staff Captain. J.R-m.
	10		Inspected the horses of 161st Brig. R.F.A. with their V.O. J.R-m.
	11	10 a.m	Inspected the animals in 95th Inf. Brig. at 3 p.m. the M.V.S. J.R-m.
	12		Capt ANDERSON A.V.C. mobilized the 219th M.S.C. Inspected animals of 96th Inf. Brig.
		2 p.m	219th Field Co R.E. & made J.P.m.s. Reint.
	13		Inspected the 219th M. Gun Co previously mobilized completed the 97th Inf. Brig. at
		2 p.m	the M.V.S. J.R-m.
	14	10 am	Inspected 157th Brig R.F.A. & 92nd Field Ambce 97th M.G. Co. J.R-m.
	15		Inspected 219 Co R.E. J.R-m.
	16		Inspected horses of 168th & Brig R.F.a.
	17		Inspected horses of Horse Battery with Brig. Gen. R.A. & 161 with Staff off J.R-m.
	18		I went to see a.D.V.S. 61st Divn. J.R-m.
	19		I inspected 168th Brig. R.F.a. & animals to be evacuated at M.V.S. J.R-m.

WAR DIARY
INTELLIGENCE SUMMARY

Vol. XVII (con.) A.D.V.S.
32nd Div.

Army Form C. 2118

Place	Date	Hour	Summary of Events and Information	Remarks and references to Appendices
AUROIR	20th		I went round the 14th Inf. Brig. 159 & 168th Brig. J. R-m.	
	21st		I went to 219th Field Co R.E. & at 2. Dinefeld 161st Brig. J.A. with Staff Captain 161st Brig. R-m.	
VOYENNE	22nd		D.H.Q. moved to VOYENNE & M.V.S. to BILLENCOURT. J. R-m.	
	23rd		I went round the Horse-G.H.Q. with new Camp Commandant & at 3 p.m. with D.A.Q.M.G. to see the 98 new Remounts. J. R-m.	
	24th		I went round all the 97th Inf. Brig. & at 2 p.m. the 96th Inf. Brig. J. R-m.	
	25th		I attended with D.A.Q.M.G. at the issuing out of Remounts at 3 p.m. I inspected the M.V.S. & 2/19th m. J.C. J. R-m.	
	26th		I went round the D.H.Q. Horses & J. R-m.	
	27th		I went round D.H.Q. with Camp Commandant. & at 2 I went round the 96th Inf. Brig. J. R-m.	
	28th		I went round all the 97th Inf. Brig. & at 2 p.m. the 14th Inf. Brig. J. R-m.	
	29th	10 a.m.	with known officers with intention of trying to arrange purchase of Cast Horses for French Farmers in situated Country. J. R-m.	
	30th		I went with D.A.D.M.C. to inspect Riders in M.V.S. with a view to transferring son reduction of Detachment. Many Horses were not properly numbered & the V.O. & N.C.O. did not know what their numbers were & the book was not corrected by Sept. at 3 p.m. I inspected the 161st & 23rd Brig. Horses R.F.A. J. R-m.	

Army Form C. 2118

WAR DIARY
or
INTELLIGENCE SUMMARY
(Erase heading not required.)

Vol 18

Confidential

War Diary
of
A.D.V.S. 32nd Division
from May 1st 1917 to May 31st 1917

Vol. XVIII

Army Form C. 2118.

WAR DIARY
INTELLIGENCE SUMMARY

A.D.V.S.
32 w Div

Vol. XVIII

(Erase heading not required.)

Place	Date	Hour	Summary of Events and Information	Remarks and references to Appendices
VOYENNE	MAY 2		Inspected M.V.S. & 20 & Co Div Train. J.R-m.	
"	3		Inspected horses of 97th Inf Brig. 219th m Gun Co & M.V.S. J.R-m	
"	4		Attended conference of A.D.V.S. & inspected M.V.S. J.R-m.	
"	5		Inspected horses in 168th Brig. R.F.A. & M.V.S. Lathouse demonstration by Gas Officer. J.R-m.	
"	6		Inspected pack of B.a.c. 14th Inf Brig. Inruelling Fusiliers 5/6 Royal Scots	
"	7		91st Field Amb & M.V.S. J.R-m.	
"	8		Inspected 219th m Gun Co & M.V.S. J.R-m.	
"	9		In stall animals & 4 of B. Squn whose being clipped. J.R-m.	
"	10		Inspected M.V.S. Lathouse demonstration by Gas officer. J.R-m.	
"	11		Inspected M.V.S. & 167 & 168 Brigades R.F.A. J.R-m.	
"	12		Inspected Pack & a.R.M.b. the mourn out Remounts inspected & 14th R.F.A. J.R-m.	
"	13		Inspected 130th M.V.S. & spent the day with D.D.V.S. J.R-m.	
"	14		Inspected M.V.S. & Saw evacuated horses entrained. J.R-m.	
"	15		Office all day. J.R-m.	
"	16	7 am	Inspected M.V.S. 1219 & Field & F.E. & 161 mtg Bing R.F.A. J.R-m.	
BEAUCOURT	17	2 p.m	Inspected M.V.S. 2168 Brig R.F.a. J.R-m.	
"			At D.Q. mode to	
"			Inspected with S.O.3 to see the 14 Inf Brig march in at	
"	18		went to see 03 161 J.R-m	
"			Inspected horses 96 Inft Brig J.R-m	
"	19		Inspected horses in Inft Brig & 161 Brig R.F.A. J.R-m.	

WAR DIARY

INTELLIGENCE SUMMARY.

(Erase heading not required.)

Army Form C. 2118.

Instructions regarding War Diaries and Intelligence Summaries are contained in F. S. Regs., Part II. and the Staff Manual respectively. Title pages will be prepared in manuscript.

Place	Date	Hour	Summary of Events and Information	Remarks and references to Appendices
	May 20.		I went to see C.R.A. & inspected Inf. Units. G.R-m.	
	21.		I superintended disinfection of men & store & blankets. Inspected M.V.S. G.R-m.	
	22.		I inspected horses in C. 16.8 d at 2 the 161 & Brig. R.L.A. G.R-m.	
	23.		I spent the day seeing the R.A. entrain. G.R-m.	
	24.		I inspected Inf. Units with Capt ANDERSON A.V.C. & also the Surplus Pack Animals with D.A.Q.M.G. G.R-m.	
	25.		I inspected A.M. Cable Section & M.V.S. & at 5 p.m the 96th Inf. Brigade. G.R-m.	
	26.		I saw 80 Carthorses posted. G.R-m.	
	27.		went round Signals & I.H.Q. G.R-m.	
	28.		Office all day. G.R-m.	
	29.		I inspected 2 of 97 Inf. Brig. G.R-m.	
	30.		I inspected the remainder of 97 Inf. Brig. G.R-m.	
	31.		I inspected some of 1st Dnft. Brig. G.R-m.	

Confidential

War Diary
of
A.D.V.S., 32nd Division

From 1st June to 30th June 1917.

(Volume XIX).

T. Rees Wigg
Major.
D.A.D.V.S.
32nd Div.

Army Form C. 2118.

Instructions regarding War Diaries and Intelligence Summaries are contained in F.S. Regs., Part II. and the Staff Manual respectively. Title pages will be prepared in manuscript.

WAR DIARY
of A.D.V.S. 32 w Div.

Vol XIX INTELLIGENCE SUMMARY.

(Erase heading not required.)

Place	Date	Hour	Summary of Events and Information	Remarks and references to Appendices
BEFAU COURT	June 1		D.H.Q. moved to VIEUX BERQUIN. T.R-m.	
	2		I went round 96th Inf Brig & at 3 p.m. to see the D.D.V.S. 2nd Army. T.R-m.	
	3		I went round the 14th & 97 Inf Brigades. T.R-m.	
VIEUX BERQUIN	4		I went round the Signals & Am. D.D.V.S. came to see me. T.R-m.	
	5		I went round some of the 14th & 97th Inf. Brig. & inspected horses to be evacuated in M.V.S. T.R-m.	
	6		I worked in all day arising payment re the R.A. T.R-m.	
	7		I third Thursday with the 161 & 168 R.A. Brigades. T.R-m.	
	8		I inspected the M.V.S. I went to see the Corps Dipping Baths. I went to see a.D.V.S. 36 w Div. T.R-m.	
	9		I went to see some of the 96w Inf. Brig. T.R-m.	
	10		I went round Units arranging for the Use of Dipping Baths & inspected M.V.S. T.R-m.	
	11		I inspected some of the 97 Inf Brig and the H.Q. T.R-m.	
	12		I went to see the 2 cases floated & horses evacuated. Then inspected the M. Det Eng. T.R-m.	
	13		I went to see D.D.V.S. & No 7 Vet. Hosp. T.R-m.	
	14		I went with D.A.Q.M.G. to met the Remounts. T.R-m.	
	15		D.H.Q. moved to F.R-m.	
MORBER	16		I inspected M.V.S. T.R-m.	
CAE	17		I inspected M.V.S. T.R-m.	
TRAMSCHE	18		I inspected M.V.S. & D.A.C. & A.L.C. Bts 168. T.R-m.	

WAR DIARY
INTELLIGENCE SUMMARY
(Erase heading not required.)

Army Form C. 2118.

X / X   A.D.V.S. 32nd Div

Place	Date	Hour	Summary of Events and Information	Remarks and references to Appendices
COXIDE	19		I went to Coxyde to see the A.D.V.S. I visited the M.V.S. & D.A.C. 7 p.m.	
	20		D.H.Q. moved to 5 p.m.	
L.F.S	21		I inspected 2 Farm Inf. Units & M V.S. & D 168 & C 161 & after tea	
	~~22~~		a L.B. Batteries 161. 5 p.m.	
BAINS	22		I inspected the M. Gun Corps. 5 p.m.	
	23		I visited some R.A. Units & M.V.S. & D 168. 5 p.m.	
	24		Went to see the 96th Inf. Brig. 5 p.m.	
	25		Went round with the I.O. the 14 & 97 Inf. Brig & M.V.S. 7 p.m.	
	26		I visited 1 & 2 Section D.A.C. & at 2 to 3 Section 5 p.m.	
	27		I visited 96 Inf. Brig. & some 60 Battery 168 & some 7 p.m.	
	28		I saw C 168 & B 161 & Signal Co. 5 p.m.	
	29		20 cases evacuated by road. I visited some of the Batteries. 7 p.m.	
	30		I helped test C. Battery 168 & visited M.V.S. 7 p.m.	

Army Form C. 2118.

WAR DIARY
or
INTELLIGENCE SUMMARY.

(Erase heading not required.)

Vol XX

Confidential War Diary of
D.A.D.V.S. 32nd Div.
from July 1st — July 31st 17

E. Road Morgan
Major.
D.A.D.V.S.
32nd Div.

Army Form C. 2118.

Vol XX

WAR DIARY
or
INTELLIGENCE SUMMARY

D.A.D.V.S. 32nd Div

(Erase heading not required.)

Instructions regarding War Diaries and Intelligence Summaries are contained in F. S. Regs., Part II. and the Staff Manual respectively. Title pages will be prepared in manuscript.

Place	Date July	Hour	Summary of Events and Information	Remarks and references to Appendices
COXYDE	1.		Inspected horses C 188 Ambt & north problem other nipped & bowels	
LES			Inspected horses A 158 of M.V.S. I noticed 3 doubtful guns on O.B.P.	S.R-M
BAINS	2.		Inspected horses R.C. 168/Brig, R.I.A. & M.V.S.	S.R-M
	3.		Inspected horses again in R. 168. Inspected A D.V.S. Corps	S.R-M
	4.		Went to see the suspicious mange cases R.A.C. 168. & the animal to be mated in M.V.S.	
			Capt. MILLS A.V.C. was sent to 168 Bde S.	
	5.		Capt. REED to Gen. Train in addition to M.V.S.	
	6.		Inspected 3. 168 Bge R.I.A. & 97 Inf. Brig.	S.R-M
	7.		Went to see F.O.D. & 257 Tunnelling Co. R.I.	S.R-M
	8.		Attended a D.V.S. Conference. Present an order to 130 at Arr.	
			Gave Orders to Capt. REED A.V.C. to proceed to leave Inspected Section D.A.C.	S.R-M
	9.		Cancelled the orders to Capt. REED A.V.C. having received a memo from A.V.S. of the District. Inspected 2 Section D.V.S. & save great difficulty Capt. MILLS A.V.C. to be transferred & to have off. Capt REED A.V.C. to take on July charge of R. 168 Brig. in addition to his I unit to his A.D.V.S.	S.R-M
	10.		Granted one the Lieut Whear & 97 Inf. Brig. Lt/A.B.R. Brig. Capt. J.M.	
	11.		RICHARDSON M.A.C. two more men. Capt SOUTHILL A.V.C. was killed. Inspected W.P. & A.R. Capt. ADDISON M.V.C. I cancelled Capt. MILLS A.V.C.	S.R-M

Army Form C. 2118.

WAR DIARY
or
INTELLIGENCE SUMMARY.
(Erase heading not required.)

D.A.D.V.S.
32nd Div.
Vol XX

Instructions regarding War Diaries and Intelligence Summaries are contained in F. S. Regs., Part II. and the Staff Manual respectively. Title pages will be prepared in manuscript.

Place	Date	Hour	Summary of Events and Information	Remarks and references to Appendices
	12		Inspected animals in Nos 2 & 3 Section D.A.C. & at S.A Battery 168th Brig R.A.M.	
	13		Had a Conference of V.Os. A.D.V.S came to see me. Inspected 96th Inf. Brig. S.R.M.	
	14		Inspected B.169, 92nd Field Amb. of M.V.S. S.R-m.	
	15		Inspected horses in C161 & C1685 animals who evacuated M.V.S. S.R-m.	
	16		Inspected horses in 92nd Field Amb, 97th Inf. Brig. & 219th M. Gun Co. S.R-m.	
	17		Took round the A.D.V.S 49" Div. round the M.V.S. & went to see D.a.D.V.S. 49 Div.	
			Inspected horses in a 161. S.R-m.	
	18		Inspected B 161 & carried out remounts. S.R-m.	
ROSENDALE	19		Inspected horses in B 161 & B 168 & left for S.R-m	
	20		Went round all the Horses Standing Quarters & noted M.V.S. S.R-m.	
	21		Attended conference of A.D.V.S. Horses J.R-m.	
	22		Inspected all the animals of Staff 2nd & Signals. S.R-m.	
	23		Inspected M.V.S. & went to see D.D.V.S. re the transisioning Horse Inspection Corps	
	24		A D.V.S. & there Inspected 96" Inf. Brig. S.R-m.	
	25		Went over the 97th Inf. Bns. S.R-m.	
	26		Went round the 2 Inspected 96th Inf. Brig. at 2 I saw the wounded animals returning S.R-m.	
	27		Attended Conference A.D.V.S. & mentioned having 96th Inf. Brig. with the Asst Horse Master S.R-m	
	28		In office. S.R-m.	
	29		Inspected M.V.S. & met A.D.V.S. I received recommendation from C.R.A. for	
	30		a Military Cross to be given to Capt. J. M. RICHARDSON A.V.C T.F. S.R-m.	
	31		I received orders to proceed to M.V.S. & Inspite attached to I.C. 42 M.V.S. service	
			to D.A.D.V.S. 49" Div. S.R-m.	

WAR DIARY
or
INTELLIGENCE SUMMARY.

Vol XXI
Confidential War Diary
of D.a.D.V.S. 32nd Dn
from 1st Aug to 31st Aug 1917

J Rees Mogg
Major
D.a.D.V.S.
32nd Dn

Army Form C. 2118.

WAR DIARY
or
Vol XXI INTELLIGENCE SUMMARY. D.A.D.V.S. 32nd Div.

(Erase heading not required.)

Instructions regarding War Diaries and Intelligence Summaries are contained in F. S. Regs., Part II. and the Staff Manual respectively. Title pages will be prepared in manuscript.

Place	Date	Hour	Summary of Events and Information	Remarks and references to Appendices
ROSEN	Aug 1		Spent the day at No.4 Vety Hosp. CALAIS. J.R-m.	
DALE	2		Inspected M.V.S. J.R-m	
	3		D.H.Q. & D.M.V.S. moved to	
COXYDE	4		D.A.D.V.S. 49 Div came to picnic & lunch. at 4 p.m. Inspected a/s 168. J.R-m	
LES BAINS	5		Inspected a x C. Batteries 168th Brig & B/H./161st Brig. J. R-m. J.R-m.	
	6		Inspected M.V.S & C/61 & A.161. J. R-m.	
	7		a.D.V.S. attached maj. inspected the 161 & 168th Brig. R.J.a. J. R-m.	
	8		Inspected the D.a.C. J.R-m.	
	9		Lashinger & Lt R950th A.V.C. reported to H.Q. C. as an Immediate Reserve & went to B.Q. to notify to be medically examined & detachment J.R-m.	
	10		Inspected staff B & Cable Section. J.R-m.	
	11		Inspected the 96th Inf. Brig at 5 p.m. J.R-m.	
	12		I attended a D.V.S. Conference. Inspected some horses in D.A.C recently transferred to the 2 H.Q. Signals, M.R.S. & R.E. Units. J R-m	
	13		Inspected horses in A Btys 161 & B.168 & called on Eye sphe. Inst took at by of horses suffering from Opthalmia. at J inspected D.V.S. J. R-m.	
	14		Cpt MILLS A.V.C. & I went to 6 Batteries to pick out mares suitable for breeding J.R-m	
	15		Cpt MILLS A.V.C. & I went to 5 Batteries & picked out mares suitable for breeding J.R-m.	
	16		Went to see B.A.D.V.S. 33rd Div. J.R-m. J took D.a.D.V.S. Around the M.V.S. I went round the horses in Signal Co. Cable Section. J.R-m.	
	17		Inspection leave J. R-m.	

Army Form C. 2118.

WAR DIARY
INTELLIGENCE SUMMARY.

D.a.D.V.S. 32 Div
(Erase heading not required.)

Instructions regarding War Diaries and Intelligence Summaries are contained in F. S. Regs., Part II. and the Staff Manual respectively. Title pages will be prepared in manuscript.

Place	Date	Hour	Summary of Events and Information	Remarks and references to Appendices
COXYDE-LES-BAINS	18th		Divisional H.Q. moved to LA PANNE	
LA-PANNE	19th		Visited 161 & 168 Bdes R.F.A. at Office in the afternoon. JJM	
"	20th		Inspected D Batt. 168 Bde. JJM	
"	21st		At Office in the morning. Inspected a dog with suspected Rabies. JJM	
"	22nd		Inspected B. Batt. 161 Bde also C & B 168 Bde. JJM	
"	23rd		" B & C Batt. 161 Bde R.F.A. at Office in the afternoon JJM	
"	24th		" D Batt 161 Bde R.F.A. JJM	
"	25th		" A & C Batteries 161 Bde also A Batt 168 Bde. JJM	
"	26th		At Office in the morning Visited mobile Vety Sect in the afternoon JJM	
"	27th		Visited 161 Bde in the morning. At Office in the afternoon. JJM	
"	28th		With A.D.V.S. Corps. Collected manes of Artillery at a Batt. Horse show here put for horse huspiges JJM	
COXYDE-LES-BAINS	29th		Collected manes of Infantry fit for horse huspiges at that Vety Sect JJM	
"	30th		Visited Mob. Vy sect at Office in the afternoon JJM	
"	31st		Visited 168 Bde in the morning at Office during the afternoon made out weekly returns JJM	

Army Form C. 2118.

WAR DIARY
or
INTELLIGENCE SUMMARY.
(Erase heading not required.)

Vol 22

Confidential

War Diary
of
D.A.D.V.S. 32nd Division.
From Sept. 1st to Sept. 30/17.
(Volume XXII)

T. Rew Bigg
Major.
D.A.D.V.S.
32nd Div.

Army Form C. 2118.

WAR DIARY
INTELLIGENCE SUMMARY.
(Erase heading not required.)

Vol XXII D.A.D.V.S. 32nd Div.

Place	Date	Hour	Summary of Events and Information	Remarks and references to Appendices
COXYDE LES BAINS	1		Office all day. J.R-m.	
	2		R.O.P. came home. J.R-m.	
	3		Inspected horses in J.A.C. R&C Batteries 168 Bde at 5 p.m. Int. Brig J.R-m.	
	4		Inspected horses, evacuation at M.V.S. I gave a lecture to 96th Inf. Brig. Inspected horses of 16th LTMC. Jrs of Seaforth Highlanders. J.R-m.	
	5		Inspected horses in A161, B161, B14 = Inf Brig J.R-m	
	6		I went to see A.D.V.S. Inspected horses in A161 & D168 at 5 pm the 97th Inf Bde J.R-m.	
	7		Inspected M.V.S. 9th & 92nd Field Ambs. D.H. & Signals. J.R-m.	
	8		Went to conference whatever from A.D.V.S. office Sanded M.V.S. J.R-m.	
	9		I visited M.V.S. & went to A.D.V.S. office J.R-m.	
	10		Inspected horses in C161 & A168 M.Dro 161 & H.2 Hvo 168 2.M.V.S.	
	11		I attended A.D.V.S.'s office J.R-m	
	12		I went to see 206 & 20 R.E. 13 killed & 13 wounded & Went to Railhead to see horses for entraining. Sent to M.V.S. & Corps. J.R-m.	
	13		Inspected 14th Inf. Brig. & M.V.S. & Div. Train & A.D.V.S. office & went round at 8 p.m. I distributed the Remounts. J.R-m.	
	14		Inspected the Pioneer Batt & Report of 97th Machine Gun Co & met DD.V.S. at M.V.S.	
	15		Inspected M.V.S. & A.D.V.S. office 2nd Army & saw DD.V.S. J.R-m.	
	16		Inspected M.V.S. & T.P.O.P. at Corps. Inspected M.V.S. J.R-m.	
	17		Attended at Conference A.D.V.S. office J.R-m.	
	18		Visited M.V.S. 161 & 97 Int. Inf. I visited M.V.S. & A.D.V.S. office J.R-m.	
			Inspected A 161, 92 M.V.S. J. Railhead to see horses travelled to A.D.V.S. office J.R-m.	
			Inspected Signals Sub Railhead J.R-m.	

Army Form C. 2118.

WAR DIARY
or
INTELLIGENCE SUMMARY.
(Erase heading not required.)

Vol XXII (con)   D.A.D.M.S.
                 32nd Div.

Place	Date	Hour	Summary of Events and Information	Remarks and references to Appendices
	19		Visited M.V.S. & B's & C Batteries 168. Visited A.D.M.S. office & handed in an official complaint to A. & Q.M.G. enclosing him War office letter No. 17/1630 (A.S.) dated 22nd July 1915 & D.V.S. letter No. 3/2984/50 dated 14/8/15 that I had the greatest difficulty & much unpleasantness in getting a Cert. of a 15 year Reg. pony by A.D. & Q.M.G. who informed me that though I gave long enough notice for him in future that I always go in straight for what I felt was wrong not doubts arise in future. Inspected many units & R-m.	
	20		Same Cad. Inspected 5/6 Argyl Scots to A/1 & Field Amb & M.V.S. & 161, 4th Amm. Res. Transport & R-m.	
	21		Visited No2 Vet D.A.C. & M.V.S. & R-m.	
	22		Visited Signals M.V.S. & R-m.	
	23		Inspected & arranged evacuation of 161 & D.A.C. & M.	
	24		Visited M.V.S. & Evacuated to Railhead completed evacuation 96 & 219 m. Jan 6, & R-m.	
	25		Inspected 17th-19th Inf. Brig. at 3 Divisioned out the Remounts & R-m.	
	26		Visited M. F.E. & D 161. & R-m.	
	27		Visited A.D.M.S. H/2 Div. & 3 Coys R.E. & M.Y.S. at 2 Inspections	
	28		Inspected see D.A.D.V.S. conference & inspected A 161 & #2 D 148 & J R.E. & R-m	
	29		Visited M.V.S. went to A.D.V.S. Conference & inspected A 160 & B 168 & R-m. Inspected A 160 & B 168 & R-m.	
	30		Inspected M.V.S. & R-m.	

Army Form C. 2118.

WAR DIARY
or
INTELLIGENCE SUMMARY.
(Erase heading not required.)

WA 23

Confidential
War Diary
of
D.A.D.V.S. 32nd Division
From 1st to 31st October 1917.

Volume XXIII

G. Rees Mogg
Major
D.A.D.V.S.
32nd Division

Army Form C. 2118.

WAR DIARY
INTELLIGENCE SUMMARY.
(Erase heading not required.)

Vol. 23 D.A.D.V.S. 32nd Divn

Place	Date	Hour	Summary of Events and Information	Remarks and references to Appendices
COXYDE	Oct 1		Inspected M.V.S. Hant of 96th Inf. Brig. & rest D.a D.V.S. 41st Div	G.R-m.
LES	2		Went to Railhead & saw horses entrained & inspected 2nd Manchesters M.S.R.M	G.R-m.
BAINS	3		Inspected 92nd Field Amb. M/1 Fd G. M.V.S. from L.V.R. Cable Section	G.R-m.
	4		Gathering & Carting parties D.S.R.	G.R-m.
	5		D.a.D.V.S. 42nd Div came to see me re taking over	G.R-m.
	6		Went with Capt J.J. MILLS A.V.C. by train to	G.R-m.
			to receive the mule agricole from the French minister of agriculture	G.R-m.
ARRAS	7		Returned to S.R-m.	
	8			
COXYDE	9		A.D.V.S. came to see me & pm off. I went to him to get a new form for the M.V.S. to fill in etc.	G.R-m.
	10		M.V.S. moved to new area. I inspected 168th Brig L.B. 168.	G.R-m.
LA PANNE	11		Went to see D.a.D.V.S. 41st 242nd Div D.H.Q. moved.	G.R-m.
ROSENDALE	12		I inspected M.V.S.	G.R-m.
	13		I went round the 97th Brig.	G.R-m.
	14		Office all day.	G.R-m.
	15		I inspected M.V.S. & saw some of the 161st & 168th Brigades.	G.R-m.
	16		I went round the 96th Inf. Brig.	G.R-m.
	17		I went round some of the ———— 14th Inf. Brig.	G.R-m.
	18		I went round the rest of the 14th Inf. Brig.	G.R-m.
	19		I arranged about the new tanks for chaff cutters & inspected the 14th Sqn Brig. M. Gun C.	G.R-m.

Army Form C. 2118.

WAR DIARY D.A.D.V.S.
Vol. 23 ~~am~~ INTELLIGENCE SUMMARY. 32nd Div.

(Erase heading not required.)

Place	Date	Hour	Summary of Events and Information	Remarks and references to Appendices
	Oct. 20		I attended Conference at Corps. J. R-m.	
	21		I went to M.V.S. J. R-m.	
	22		Office in mrn. Went to see D.D.V.S. in aft. J. R-m.	
	23		D.H.Q. moved to J. R-m.	
LE CLIPBM	24		Inspected none of 14th Inf. Brig. J. R-m.	
	25		Office. Nothing to report. J. R-m.	
	26		D.H.Q. moved to J. R-m.	
LEDERZEELE	27		I inspected M.V.S. & went to No. 23 Vety Hosp. J. R-m.	
	28		I inspected M.V.S. J. R-m.	
	29		I inspected M.V.S. J. R-m.	
	30		I inspected M.V.S. J. R-m.	
	31		I inspected horses of 96th Inf. Brig. J. R-m.	

Army Form C. 2118.

WAR DIARY
or
INTELLIGENCE SUMMARY.

(Erase heading not required.)

Vol. 25
Confidential War Diary
of
D.A.D.V.S. 32nd Div.

From 1st — 30th Nov. 1917.

by Major G. Keogh M.R.C.V.S.
D.A.D.V.S.
32nd Div.

WAR DIARY
or
INTELLIGENCE SUMMARY.

Army Form C. 2118.

D.A.D.V.S. 32nd Div.
Vol. 25

D.V. No. 2903
32nd DIVISION

Instructions regarding War Diaries and Intelligence Summaries are contained in F.S. Regs., Part II. and the Staff Manual respectively. Title pages will be prepared in manuscript.

(Erase heading not required.)

Place	Date	Hour	Summary of Events and Information	Remarks and references to Appendices
LEDER ZEELE	Nov 1		Inspected horses for evacuation in M.V.S. 215th 96th Lanc. Fus. T.R-m.	
	2		Inspected M.V.S. orders arrived for Capt. MILLS to go to W. Ray Horse T.R-m.	
	3		I visited part of 14th Inf. Bng. T.R-m.	
	4		M.V.S. march to 96th Regt. area T.R-m.	
	5		I visited the remainder of 14th Inf. Bng. Capt. Mc MAHON a.v.c. arrived T.R-m.	
	6		I took Capt. McMAHON R.V.C. to the Artillery & saw the 168th Bng. R.F.A. & 2 D.A.C.'s	
			58th Div. & a DHQ II Corps. T.R-m.	
	7		A.D.V.S. XVIII Corps came to see me T.R-m.	
	8		I went to see the A.A. & Q.M.G. about an official complaint which had	
			been made about T.R-m.	
	9		I visited the 97th Inf. Bng. T.R-m.	
	10		Office all day T.R-m.	
	11		D.H.Q. moved. I went to see new billets T.R-m.	
POPER INGHE	12		I went to see horses entrained for evacuation to Base T.R-m.	
	13		Inspected M.V.S. new billet T.R-m.	
	14		Inspected M.V.S. & mentioned the S.A. & A. batteries 168th Bng. R.F.A.	
	15		Inspected 15 & 2 D. Batteries 168th L.M.V.S. T.R-m.	
	16		I went round 151st & 160th Bng. R.F.A. T.R-m.	
	17		I saw & saw D.A.D.V.S. 8th Div. I went round the M.V.S. T.R-m.	
	18		A.A. & Q.M.G. mentioned the M.V.S. T.R-m.	
	19		I attended execution of horses at Railhead T.R-m.	

Army Form C. 2118.

WAR DIARY
or
INTELLIGENCE SUMMARY.
(Erase heading not required.)

Vol 25(cm) of D.A.D.R.S. 32 w Div.

Place	Date	Hour	Summary of Events and Information	Remarks and references to Appendices
POPER INGHE	20		I went to see D.A.D.R.S. 1st Div. re taking over about 2 m 3/3 35-gu. and m.V.S. of A.D.V.S. I Corps. 5. R-m.	
			Inspected m.V.S. of 32nd + 6th. M.V.S. J. R-m	
	21		Inspected 6.1217 North Sec. J. R-m	
	22		I visited the Railhead. J. R-m	
	23		I went to Railhead saw 18 horses evacuated. J. R-m.	
	24		D.H.Q. moved to BRAKE CAMP. I attended Conference + took orders. J. R-m.	
BRAKE CAMP	25		Stiffened Epizootic Lymphangitis. J. R-m.	
	26		M.V.S. moved. J. R-m. I inspected M.V.S. in afternoon. J. R-m.	
	27		Office all day. Major Finlayson. J. R-m.	
	28		Inspected M.V.S. J. R-m.	
	29		I superintended the entraining of 160 horses evacuated. J. R-m.	
	30		Office all day. J. R-m.	
			Inspected E. J. R-m.	

Army Form C. 2118.

WAR DIARY
or
INTELLIGENCE SUMMARY.
(Erase heading not required.)

Vol 25

Confidential

War Diary
of
D.A.D.V.S. 32nd Division
From Dec 1st to Dec 31st 1917.

(Volume XXV).

Army Form C. 2118.

WAR DIARY
or
INTELLIGENCE SUMMARY. Vol XXV of D.A.D.V.S. 3rd M Div
(Erase heading not required.)

Place	Date	Hour	Summary of Events and Information	Remarks and references to Appendices
BASE CAMP	Dec 1		Office all day. F.R.m.	
	2		Inspected animals at M.S. F.a. Sea sickness & half mutiny by to F.a from	
	3		Went to Railhead & saw animals entrained and up to F.a. F.R.m	
	4		16 tons. Reid F.R.m. Went round hospital & Cat B & the 10.8.F.A & at a F.a from [next?] of 500 to 1st F.E.A. & 2 Italians & 150. Lew. off the	
	5		animals for evacuation at M.r.S. F.R.m	
	6		Inspected the Antisera Root Bolano & F.a of 16 R.m.	
	7		I understood 134 horses being shifted. F.R.m.	
	8		I ascertained 244 animals being shifted. Arrived on 10 F.R.m	
	9		Capt ANDERSON A.V.C. F.R.m. Left at 9 a.m. F.R.m.	

Army Form C. 2118.

WAR DIARY
INTELLIGENCE SUMMARY

of J.A. + A.L.S.
32nd Division

(Erase heading not required.)

Instructions regarding War Diaries and Intelligence Summaries are contained in F. S. Regs., Part II. and the Staff Manual respectively. Title Pages will be prepared in manuscript.

Place	Date	Hour	Summary of Events and Information	Remarks and references to Appendices
	10.12.16		Visited office	wa.
	11.		" units	wa.
	12.		" "	wa.
	13.		" office	wa.
	14.		" " + interview at O. office	wa.
	15.		" units + visited M.O.S.	wa.
	16.		" office	wa.
	17.		" units	wa.
	18.		" "	wa.
	19.		" office	wa.
	20.		" units	wa.
	21.		" "	wa.
	22.		" office	wa.
	23.		" office	wa.
	24.		" units + office	wa.

W. Anderson Capt. R.A.S.C.
acting D.A.A.S. 32nd Div.

Army Form C. 2118.

Instructions regarding War Diaries and Intelligence Summaries are contained in F. S. Regs., Part II. and the Staff Manual respectively. Title pages will be prepared in manuscript.

WAR DIARY
or
INTELLIGENCE SUMMARY.
(Erase heading not required.)

J.a.D.V.S
32 rd Div

Vol XXV

Place	Date	Hour	Summary of Events and Information	Remarks and references to Appendices
	24		In Office — J. R-m	
	25		In Office. J.R-m	
	26		Went upon a.a.D Ban.tesis 168 & 3.ng Bat 3 Veloc. te	
	27		M.V.S. 6. R-m.	
	28		Lunch w/c a.D.V.S who motor'd with D.D.V.S to see the	
			M.V.S. J.R.-m.	
	29		In Office. J. R-m.	
	30		Capt Offied came of prison D.H.Q. moved to	
LUTKE	31		New place. J. M.V.S. J.R-m.	
GUEL				

WAR DIARY
or
INTELLIGENCE SUMMARY
(*Erase heading not required.*)

Army Form C. 2118.

Confidential

War Diary
of
D.A.D.V.S., 32nd Division
From January 1st to Janry 31st 1918.

(Volume XXVI)

T. Kev Mogg.
MAJOR
D.A.D.V.S.
32nd DIVISION.

Army Form C. 2118.

WAR DIARY D.A.D.V.S.
OF
INTELLIGENCE SUMMARY. 32nd Div.

Vol. 26.

(Erase heading not required.)

Place	Date	Hour	Summary of Events and Information	Remarks and references to Appendices
ZOTTREUX	Jany 1, 2		Went to BOULOGNE. F.R.M.	
	2nd		Visited No 3 Vety Hospital & pour Th. Mange #336 3 Chambon. F. R-M.	
	3		Inspected mounted M.P.S. F.R.M.	
	4		Handed over to Capt. ANDERSON A.V.C. went to II Corps. F R-M.	
7.K.RC 31.18	5th		At office & visited units (R)	
	6th		Visited units. W.A.	
	7th		do. W.A.	
	8th		do. W.A.	
	9th		do. W.A.	
	10th		At office & visited units W.A.	
	11th		Visited units W.A.	
	12th		do. W.A.	
	13th		At office do. W.A.	
	14th		do. W.A.	
	15th		do. W.A.	

Army Form C. 2118.

WAR DIARY
or
INTELLIGENCE SUMMARY.

(Erase heading not required.)

Vol 26.   D.A.D.V.S. 32nd Divn

Place	Date	Hour	Summary of Events and Information	Remarks and references to Appendices
ZUTKERKE	16.1.19		Visit units. W9.	
	17th		do - W9	
	18th		do - W9	
	19th		do - W9	
	20th		do - W9	
	21st		do - "	
	22nd		Apr 9 - do - W9	
	23rd		" do "	
	24th		Returned from Leave 8 p.m.	
	25th		Went to 96 Bde & Artillery add 2 Inf Bdes & 2 Sub Sections 68 Bde 5 FA & 10 F. R-M	
	26th		Inspected the range Dep. M.g. 8 p.m. F.A.M.	
	27th		Visited the " Standing " Pos of 18 Divisions at the 97 & 2nd Inf Bdes. 5 p.m.	
	28th		Instructed the O.C. 42 M.V.S. LeMerge 5 p.m.	
	29th		Inspected the S/G ROYAL SCOTS doing the A.A. & O.M.G. 5 p.m.	
	30th		Went to see D.A.D.V.S. 18 Divn 5 p.m.	
ELVER.	31.		Inspected animals of 1st Section D.A.C. 2.30 & to Gen Train from D moved to B.150 & 257 Funneling Co. 5 R-M. Graded 42 M.V.S. R.O.Y.L.D	
DINGHE				

Army Form C. 2118.

WAR DIARY
or
INTELLIGENCE SUMMARY.
(Erase heading not required.)

Confidential
War Diary
of
D.A.D.V.S. 32nd Division.
From Feb 1st to 28th 1918.

(Volume XXVII)

J. Rees Mogg.
MAJOR
D.A.D.V.S.
32nd DIVISION.

Army Form C. 2118.

WAR DIARY
or
INTELLIGENCE SUMMARY.
(Erase heading not required.)

D.A.D.V.S. 32nd Div.

Vol 27.

Place	Date	Hour	Summary of Events and Information	Remarks and references to Appendices
ELVER DINGHE	Feby 1		1. I inspected Units with Capt. REED A.V.C. J. R-m.	
	2.		I attended Conference at Corps & on 10/2/18 Capt. McMAHON A.V.C. at Cassel. Clearing Station. J. R-m.	
	3.		I inspected Units in R.A. J. R-m.	
	4.		I superintended 380 horses being dipped & visited a Unit & took return to A.A. & Q.M.G. at night. J. R-m.	
	5.		I superintended most of 32d Horses being dipped & visited M.V.S. & here I met the A.D.V.S. 2 Corps J. R-m.	
	6.		I inspected 357 animals dipped & visited M.V.S. J. R-m.	
	7.		I took Capt. SMITH round the 2 Brigades & gave a lecture on Scab change as a temporary measure. J. R-m.	
	8.		I visited hdqrs of Stationary Division. I asked Corps Car but could not get one. Went to see O.C. W2 M.V.S. & D.A.D.V.S. 1st Dv. & 42 M.V.S. horses & 14 ts Inf Brigade. J. R-m.	
	9.		I was taken in Car to D.A.V.S. 35th Div Conference at Corps. I went to see O.C. 127 A.V.C. ie the Mange in this unit. J. R-m.	
	10.		I took Capt TOPPS A.V.C. to see Capt SMITH who took him round the 85 Batteries Iwent to see the Sick Train Used a Conference Visited my V.O.P. re dippers the strands necks & withers of animals so as to enable the early diagnosis of Mange to take place I took Return to A.A & Q.M.G. at night. J. R-m.	
	11.		I went round Dip & 2 M.G. Coys & saw the 97.M.L. 2 M.L.S. & J. R-m.	
	12.		I inspected Units in R.A. to arrange Troughs for Dipping. J. R-m.	

Army Form C. 2118.

WAR DIARY
INTELLIGENCE SUMMARY.

D.A.D.V.S.
32nd Div.
2nd (Corps)

(Erase heading not required.)

Instructions regarding War Diaries and Intelligence Summaries are contained in F.S. Regs., Part II. and the Staff Manual respectively. Title pages will be prepared in manuscript.

Place	Date	Hour	Summary of Events and Information	Remarks and references to Appendices
	Jan 12			
	13		I inspected M.V.S. & superintended dipping. T.R.M.	
	14		I superintended dipping all day. T.R.M.	
	15		I superintended dipping all day. T.R.M.	
	16		Went in a Lorry to a Corps V.C. Conference. I could not get a Conf. I inspected a 168 & all the a.v.c. Sergeants Walker take D.A.D.V.S. to Conference. I inspected the Remounts. T.R.M.	
	17		I inspected animals of the evacuated & worked out the Remounts. T.R.M.	
	18		Capt HOPPS a.V.S. came to see me re HERNIA. I inspected Labour & R.E. Units. T.R.M.	
	19		I asked for a Car but could not get one. I inspected most of the 14th & 96th S.V.S. inspected the M.V.S. T.R.M. Got Brigadier. At 2-30 the D.A.Q.M.G. went with me round the 206th & To R.E. & 193rd & Co. Div. Train & met with D.A.Q.M.G. but could not get one. T.R.M.	
	20		I asked for a Car at 2 and could not get one. I reviewed the Horses M.V.S. I examined the Equipment of all the 13 Batteries recipping at 2. I inspected the train. T.R.M.	
	21		I went with Maller's F.R.M. Train T.R.M.	
	22		I inspected M.V.S. with Horses Batteries. Train T.R.M.	
	23		I asked for Car to take me to Conference but could not get one. I inspected artillery horses working in Div. Train & horses of evacuation at M.V.S. & pond of the Batteries. T.R.M.	
	24		I got to Conference. T.R.M.	
	25		I inspected all the Batteries re dipping. I asked D.A.D.V.S. II Corps F.R.M. to let me inspect all the Infantry & artillery pond of the Batteries. T.R.M.	
	26		I inspected pond of the Batteries & latter re went & a D.V.S. II Corps F.R.M.	
	27		I inspected some of the Batteries and to latter re went & a D.V.S. II Corps F.R.M.	
	28		I inspected Infantry D.V.S. & Corps Horse Show came to see me & inspected all the Infantry animals. T.R.M.	

WAR DIARY
or
INTELLIGENCE SUMMARY.

(Erase heading not required.)

Army Form C. 2118.

Confidential

War Diary
of
D.A.D.V.S. 32nd Division.

From Mar 1st to Mar. 31st 1918.

(Volume 29)

F. Revs Mogg.
MAJOR
D.A.D.V.S.
32nd DIVISION.

Army Form C. 2118.

WAR DIARY
or
INTELLIGENCE SUMMARY.
(Erase heading not required.)

Vol. 29   D.A.D.V.S. 32nd Div.

Place	Date	Hour	Summary of Events and Information	Remarks and references to Appendices
EL VER DINGHE	MAR 1		Went to No 42 M.V.S. & found Capt. D.V. REED A.V.C. not finished dressing an 9-30. Had three previously spoke to him about not being out earlier. Gave instructions horses to be out and fed. Mange dept. & foot instructions horses to be clipped add 9-30 every day. Inspected the mange dept. 500 animals were clipped. To R-m.	
	2		I was all the day at Mange Dept. 500 were clipped. To R-m.	
	3		Went round all the Batteries in morn. & to & weekly returns & any reports to a A.D.V.S. & Capt. Horse adviser inspected to R.A. forges. To R-m.	
	4		a A.D.V.S. & Capt. Horse adviser inspected to R.A. forges. To R-m. a/c a 2 inspected stables & officer in morn. No mention [?] of N.C.O. a V.C.	
	5		Saw the a.a. Q.M.G. re Capt D.V. REED A.V.C. not obeying orders. Batteries in morn. Capt D.V. REED A.V.C. that he was not to forward his indents to me in future. Capt D.V. REED A.V.C. at NADA for 2 months. To R-m.	
	6		appearances for 6 weeks Sent to No 10 C 161 attend R.Y.A. Rode a lot of Island horses. To R-m.	
	7		Went to dep at Mange Dept. in evening. Inspected the M.V.S. To R-m.	
	8		Went to day at Mange Dept. To R-m.	
	9		Inspected horses of the Batteries Weekly return & reports to a a D.V.S. at night. To R-m.	
	10		a a D.V.S. A.V.C. round the animals of 306 & 219 OR E. 290 Field Amb. Sat 2 p.m. Went round with the O.C. the Batteries Conferences the m. angles.	
	11		Capt D.V. REED A.V.C. was informed by the a a D.M.S. Inspected the r. angles Sutherland 1/5/6 Royal Scots well also 2nd Brig Sat 2 p.m. an 2 Batteries 161 Brigade RFA	
	12		Went round Batteries. To R-m.	
	13			

Army Form C. 2118.

WAR DIARY
or
INTELLIGENCE SUMMARY.
(Erase heading not required.)

J.A.D.V.S.
32 [?]

Instructions regarding War Diaries and Intelligence
Summaries are contained in F. S. Regs., Part II.
and the Staff Manual respectively. Title pages
will be prepared in manuscript.

Place	Date	Hour	Summary of Events and Information	Remarks and references to Appendices
ELVER DINGHE	14th		Inspected the mingalion M. Gun Park & distributed 82 Remounts to R-m.	
	15th		I met A.D.V.S. who inspected the H.Q. Blind horses at 1/10 M.V.S. & went on to see	
			the 158th Bde & J.A.J.R.m.	
	16th		I spent all the morning swimming in the lightwater. He did the eyes of the A.S.	
			Blind horses of R-m.	
	17th		Inspected horses in D 168 & B 181. Took routine & weekly report to A.D.V.S. F.R.m.	
	18th		Went to see Staff Captain R.A. & in aft. Inspected some of the Batteries.	
	19th		Office all day F.R.m.	
	20th		Inspected M.S. animals for No 2 makers & took north Q. Sun train to R-m.	
	21st		Inspected Conference of A.D.V.S., D.V.S. men present. I numbers No 22 Vety Hosp. F.R.m.	
	22nd		Attended Conference of A.D.V.S.'s. D.V.S. Horses entrained at VESSEL HOEK. F.R.m.	
	23rd		A.D.V.S. asked me to go & see Capt Smith-Dorrien. I at 2 p.m. I went by no 6	
			Ambulance train in 91st Field Amb. M. Gm. Capt Dorrien. F.R.m.	
			Ambulance to visiting the Munga Bdgn. F. R.m.	
			Batteries. I went over the 3 3rd Batts to Transport left by the 35th Bn. I took my weekly returns	
	24th		& went over to A.D.M.S. & R-m.	
	25th		Went to office in morning. Mange Bde. F. R.m.	
	26th		Inspected the mange bathe. F.R.m.	
	27th		In office all day. R-m.	
	28th		Made arrangement with Capt Smith are to move I went to M.V.S. F R-m	
	29th		I went to M.V.S. in office & then to D.H.Q. to report animal No. ADVS returned seem sent to	
HERMA VILLE	30th		Went to lyds & Bdn to report my animal. & to D.V.S. F R-m.	
	30th		BOULOGNE with 3rd Saphir & Nov. & tho.M.V.S. F.R.m.	
	31st		Visited No. 3 A.P.V.S. No. 3 D.V.S. & two M.V.S. F R-m.	
			Inspected M.V.S. D.H.Q. morl (arrangements only) F. R.m.	

Army Form C. 2118.

WAR DIARY
or
INTELLIGENCE SUMMARY.
(Erase heading not required.)

Instructions regarding War Diaries and Intelligence Summaries are contained in F.S. Regs., Part II. and the Staff Manual respectively. Title pages will be prepared in manuscript.

Place	Date	Hour	Summary of Events and Information	Remarks and references to Appendices

Vol 29

Confidential War Diary
of
D.A.D.V.S.
32nd Div.

From 1st April to 30th April 1918

by Ryan Major

(Volume 28)

MAJOR
D.A.D.V.S.
32nd DIVISION.

WAR DIARY
or
INTELLIGENCE SUMMARY.
(Erase heading not required.)

Army Form C. 2118.

Vol. 28. D.A.D.V.S. 32nd Div.

Place	Date	Hour	Summary of Events and Information	Remarks and references to Appendices
HERMA-VILLE HUTMENT CAMP	April 1/23		Rear D.H.Q & 42 M.V.S. moved to T.R-m.	
	2		Saw the R.A. go through & visited M.V.S. and looked animals in most of the Inf. Brigades. T. R-m.	
	3		Inspected M.V.S. T. R-m	
	4		Took the weekly Returns & Report to the A.A. & D.M.S. & T.R.M.	
	5		Visited M.V.S. Received orders to move to Rear D.H.Q T.R.m.	
	6		Inspected M.V.S. on animals Cdy's turn in & Sanit'n on the	
MONDI- COURT			was present at the Bomb. on amm'n Col's turn in & Sanit'n on the 151st Inf. Bdy all day. T. R-m.	
	7		Ditto 96th Inf Bdy. T. R-m	
	8		Ditto 97th Inf. Bdy. T. R-m.	
	9		Ditto Pioneer Battalion O.C. Bn's Instruction. T. R-m.	
	10		Inspected animals for Evacuation at M.V.S. T. R-m. vsng R.T.A. E.V.M.	
	11		Inspected the horses in D.ech Wagon lines of 161-168 T.R.m.	
	12		Inspected the Horses in D.ech Wagon lines Bdys 151-158 Tant R.T.A. E.Vet	
	13		The O.C. 161 & O.C. 168 T.H.Q R.T.A. T. R-m.	
	14		Attended Conference A.D.V.S. Corps. T. R-m.	
	15		Office all day. T. R-m	
			Went to a very ... animals that 339 Road Construction Co & the 72nd a T.a. Rly Coy. 3 Batteries had horses nearly all of them in the open & without shelter had all the horses & mules of one Battery taken to Ranschelles left to make a this ... and put animals & all the men nearly too Ranschelles leaving Major Reeves with of animals & all the men nearly too Ranschelles leaving Major B.V.S. (W.?) to see that tents & others were erected & whether it did	

Instructions regarding War Diaries and Intelligence Summaries are contained in F. S. Regs., Part II. and the Staff Manual respectively. Title pages will be prepared in manuscript.

Vol. 28 (cn)

WAR DIARY
or
INTELLIGENCE SUMMARY.
(Erase heading not required.)

D.A.D.V.S.
32nd Div

Army Form C. 2118.

Place	Date	Hour	Summary of Events and Information	Remarks and references to Appendices
MONDI COURT	16th		Office all day. G. R-M.	
	17th		I inspected the animals in the 14th Inf. Brig. & found that the watering arrangements were bad so I went to see the D.A.Q.M.G. about the matter & telephoned to the C.R.E. Corps. I inspected M.V.S. G. R-M.	
"			I went to see the horses in 96th & 97th Inf. Brig & inspected M.V.S. G. R-M.	
"	18th		Office all day. G. R-M.	
"	19th		Inspected animals for evacuation in M.V.S. & then attended Conference at Corps. I inspected animals in 96th Brig. Inf. G. R-M.	
"	20th		I got inoculated.	
"	21st		Indoors all day. Seedy. G. R-M.	
"	22nd		I went round some of the horses in rear artillery wagon lines. G. R-M.	
"	23rd		I went round the animals in 31st D.A.C. Took returns to D.A.Q.M.G. & saw the 56 remounts on way back. G. R-M. I went round animals of the 31st Div. artillery with their Staff Officer. G. R-M.	
"	24th		G. R-M. I inspected M.V.S.	
	25th		D.H.Q. moved to	
RAVIN COURT	26th		Office all day. G. R-M.	
"	27th		I attended Conference at Corps & inspected 5 Unit transport in aft. G. R-M.	
"	28th		I sent in a Report to the A.A. & Q.M.G. that as I had sent out 5 Sections of Notes on animal management during the last 2 years & 3 months & had given about 30 lectures that I did not think it was necessary for him to send round other lectures by a T.O. of considerable experience. G. R-M. I inspected 5 Inf. Transports & saw Capt REED & Capt WILSON A.V.C. G. R-M.	
	29th		O.C. M.V.S. came to see me re KINNEALY'S Court Martial. G. R-M.	
	30th		I went to see A.D.V.S. Corps & Capt. ANDERSON A.V.C. G. R-M.	

(A7092). Wt. W12839/M1293. 750,000. 1/17. D. D. & L., Ltd. Forms/C.2118/14.

WAR DIARY
or
~~INTELLIGENCE SUMMARY~~
(Erase heading not required.)

Army Form C. 2118.

Vol 30

Confidential
War Diary
of
D.A.D.V.S., 32nd Division
From May 1st to May 31st 1918.

(Volume 30)

J. Rees M__

MAJOR
D.A.D.V.S.
32nd DIVISION.

WAR DIARY
or
INTELLIGENCE SUMMARY.
(Erase heading not required.)

Army Form C. 2118.

D.A.D.V.S. 32nd Div.

Vol 30

Place	Date	Hour	Summary of Events and Information	Remarks and references to Appendices
BAKELIN COURT	May 1		Nothing to report. F.R.	
	2		" " " " F.R.	
	3		" " " " F.R.	
	4		" " " " F.R.	
	5		" " " " F.R.	
	6		In office all day. T.R-m.	
	7		Enrolf to see A & B Batteries 161 = Brig. R.F.A. T.R-m.	
			I went to see horses in 97th Inf Brig 161st Brig Hy Div & the Brigade & at 2 p.m. C & D Batteries 161st Brig. R.F.A. T.R-m.	
	8		I went round Nos 1 & 2 Sections D.A.C. In aft I went to see its A.V.K.S. D.A.V.S. who interviewed the VO for appointments after the war. F.R-m.	
	9		Inspected horses in all 168 = Brig. R.F.A. T.R-m.	
	10		I accompanied G.O.C. on his inspection of Inf. Transport & at 6 p.m. inspected surplus animals to be transferred to horse depôt on reorganization of the 11th Border Reg. T.R-m.	
	11		Jackinsons Conference at Corps. T.R-m.	
	12		Inspected horses of D.H.Q. Signals. T.R-m.	
	13		Inspected animals in 14th & 96th Inf Brig & found A.& S. Lad not kept. Rugs on their clipped animals & the 16th & Lans. Fus. were short of nose bags. T.R-m.	
	14th		Went round the animals of 97th Inf. Brig. T.R-m.	

WAR DIARY or INTELLIGENCE SUMMARY

Army Form C. 2118.

D. A. D. V. S.
32nd Div.

Vol 30 (con)

Place	Date	Hour	Summary of Events and Information	Remarks and references to Appendices
"	15		Inspected animals of Machine Gun Battalion. J.R-m.	
	16		Went to C/S Poly Spec Station & A.S. Inspected the animals in 3 Coy R.E. J.R.m.	
	17		Went over A.D.M.S. at advanced D.H.Q & Inspected M.V.S. J.R-m.	
	18		The M.V.S. was employed in the early morn. casualties burying & man kil. Prepared Conference at C/S & Army Corps & Rendezvous Bombing to G.S.O.1. G.R-m. Suspended Conference.	
	19		Inspected M.V.S. & forwarded the O.C. 12 M.V.S. recommendation on L/t. Scott BIRCHENALL A.V.C. for M.M. to Div.Q. J.R-m.	
	20		Judged in Horse Show. J.R-m.	
	21		Went to advanced D.H.Q & saw the A.Q.M.G. Brig. & Inspected all the horses in 168" Brig R.F.A. & the M.V.S. J.R-m.	
	22		Inspected the Gun Teams & found the horses I opined the whole of arranging 3rd R.E. J.A 2 Battles to be deepened. J.R-m.	
	23		Inspected Horses in 2 Sect D.A.C. A.D.V.Q. area. J.R-m.	
	24		Discs all day. Inspected Prints. J.R-m.	
	25		Discussed with R.L. Thompsett the Carrying of Rat bins for Horses. J.R-m.	
	26		Inspected AQ A.E.C. a.S c.e 92 Gds Divn. J.R-m.	
	27		Went round Horseson No 1, 6-5 a.s c.e per the 2 Bills were Peking m. J.R-m.	
	28		There reportedly Report to A.A & Q.M. & inspected M.V.S 2/15-H.L.I J.R-m.	
	29		the annecation 168 Brig R.F.A & Bat S the 3 Corps R.E. J.R-m.	
	30		Inspected Horses in 189 Mug R J.A 2nd D.A.C D.V.S Inph J.R-m.	
	31		Went to see the A.D.V.S 2nd Can. Div. re the 174 Bde R.F.A. Employed Horses 96" S.B. King 292" Field and looked for a Cert for Vet Dep to the Chafewie Kilometers refused. J.R-m.	

Army Form C. 2118.

WAR DIARY
~~INTELLIGENCE SUMMARY.~~
(Erase heading not required)

Instructions regarding War Diaries and Intelligence Summaries are contained in F. S. Regs., Part II. and the Staff Manual respectively. Title pages will be prepared in manuscript.

Vol 31

Confidential.

War Diary
of
D. A. D. V. S. 32ⁿᵈ Division.
From June 1ˢᵗ to June 30ᵗʰ 1918.

(Volume 31).

F. Keer Mogg.
MAJOR
D. A. D. V. S.
32nd DIVISION.

Army Form C. 2118.

WAR DIARY

D. a. D. V. S.

Vol. 31 INTELLIGENCE SUMMARY. 32nd Div.

(Erase heading not required.)

Instructions regarding War Diaries and Intelligence Summaries are contained in F. S. Regs., Part II. and the Staff Manual respectively. Title pages will be prepared in manuscript.

Place	Date	Hour	Summary of Events and Information	Remarks and references to Appendices
BAYIN COURT	June 1.		Attended Conference at Corps & inspected M.V.S. in aft. T.R.m.	
	2.		Inspected M.V.S. T.R.m.	
	3.		Inspected Vy. Units. T.R.m.	
	4.		Took weekly returns to A.A. & Q.M.G. & inspected M.V.S. T.R-m.	
	5.		Inspected animals in Gun Battalion. Met D.D.V.S. in aft. T.R-m.	
	6.		G.O.C. inspected M.V.S. T.R-m.	
	7.		Visited No 15 Vty. Hospital & inspected 42 M.V.S. T.R-m.	
	8.		Inspected horses 161 reg Bing. R.T.A. & M.V.S. T.R-m.	
	9.		Inspected M.V.S. & H.Q.Mn D.A.C. & Mor Section & No 6 V.E.S. T.R.m.	
	10.		Inspected M.V.S. & 168 "Bing. R.T.A. T.R-m.	
	11.		Inspected M.V.S. & Mor 2 & 3 Cos D.m. Train. T.R.m.	
	12.		Took returns to A.A. & Q.M.G. & inspected M.V.S. & Manchester Regt. T.R-m.	
	13.		Inspected with A.D.V.S. XV Corps C. the 3 Inf. Brigade & eat 9. T.R-m.	
	14.		Went to Remount Depot at GEZAINCOURT. T. R-m.	
	15.		Waited for Car to take me to Conference but could not get one. D.a.D.V.S. Guards Div. took me. Returned to M.V.S. & 90 & 91st Field ambulances	
	16.		Inspected horses in & Battery 161 & A/168 & examined Sgs of Sick Horses in M.V.S. T.R-m.	
	17.		Inspected M.V.S. & the horses in 14th Inf. Brig. T.R.m.	

Army Form C. 2118.

WAR DIARY or INTELLIGENCE SUMMARY.

D.a.D.V.S
Vol. 31 (con) 32nd Divn

Place	Date	Hour	Summary of Events and Information	Remarks and references to Appendices
	18		Examined eyes of blind horses at M.V.S. Sim the dark with a Auste. J.R.m.	
	19		Stock returns to A.A. & D.M.S. & distributed to remounts. J.R.m.	
	20		I visited M.V.S. & examined the 51 animals to be sent to the Remount Depot. I went to see the 400 horses to be transferred from the Corps, met the a.d.V.S. I visited the 339 a.J.R.E. & the 15" & 16" Lane. Fros. J.R.m.	
	21		I visited M.V.S. & No1 Section D.A.C. & No2 G.Sm. Train with 20 new Remounts. J.R.m.	
	22		I inspected the animals of D161 & the M.V.S. J.R.m.	
	23		at M.V.S. J.R.m.	
	24		I visited M.V.S. & Met the Jaguar DDVS & D.R. J.R.m.	
	25		Met with Capt. ANDERSON A.T.C. & re pack D168. I sent several exhibits cases from M.V.S. Spring reality (bad flexation, long legged Strangles) to Shorncliffe R.A.D.M.C. J.R.m.	
	26		I visited M.V.S. 16" H.A.J.R. & R Batt.y East & am Batt.y cast A.J.R.E. J.R.m.	
	27		I visited M.V.S. & went to Remount Depot. J.R.m.	
	28		I visited M.V.S. & 3rd Aux. Horse Transport. J.R.m.	
	29		I visited M.V.S. & attended Conference. J.R.m.	
	30		I visited M.V.S. & issued out Remounts. J.R.m.	

Army Form C. 2118.

WAR DIARY
or
INTELLIGENCE SUMMARY
(Erase heading not required.)

(Vol. 32)

Instructions regarding War Diaries and Intelligence Summaries are contained in F. S. Regs., Part II. and the Staff Manual respectively. Title pages will be prepared in manuscript.

Vol 32

Confidential

War Diary
of D.A.D.V.S. 32nd Division
from July 1st to July 31st 1918.

(Volume 32).

G. Reo Mogg.

MAJOR
D.A.D.V.S.
32nd DIVISION

Army Form C. 2118.

WAR DIARY
INTELLIGENCE SUMMARY.
(Erase heading not required.)

D.A.D.V.S. 32nd Div.

(Volume 32)

Instructions regarding War Diaries and Intelligence Summaries are contained in F. S. Regs., Part II. and the Staff Manual respectively. Title pages will be prepared in manuscript.

Place	Date	Hour	Summary of Events and Information	Remarks and references to Appendices
RAVIN COURT	July 1		I judged in a Canadian Railway Troops show 9-1 & in afternoon went to see the R.A. competitions. T.R.M.	
	2		Took weekly returns to A. & N.Q.M.G. I saw all the 3 Inf. Brigade Transports. In aft I judged the 155th A.T.a. Brigade elimination class. T.R.M.	
	3		I inspected m.r.s. in morning. Stood near stock or Eye diseases. At 2 I went to see the transport of 2nd Batt. Manchesters & 92nd Field Amb. & 1st Quarter to Div. train. T.R.M.	
	4		I inspected m.r.s. Stood near Stock on Eye diseases. At 2 I went to see the 96th Bring B.T.a. Transports & 40 Div. train. T.R.M.	
	5		I went to see the Transports of 218 & 219th A.T.R.E. & 2 Sections of 10 D.A. Cable exceptionally fine lot. Then Quarter to 40 Div. train. T.R.M.	
	6		I went round the lines on 168th Brig. R.F.A. ambulances &c. T.R.M.	
	7		I went to pay the animals K.O.Y.L.I. I gave them a chaff cutter. Remounts arrived at 9 p.m. a good lot. T.R.M.	
	8		I had sore throat on Eyes in morning. Div. apt went to see Transport of B 188 Nos Section D.A.C. 92 Field Amb. Headquarters D.A.C & 12 Batt. Manchesters T.R.M.	
	9		I inspected m.r.s. sore throat & Eyes. T.R.M.	
	10		I was at Conference. Unwell day. T.R.M.	
	11		I inspected animals Signals & A. T.R.M.	

Army Form C. 2118.

WAR DIARY
or
INTELLIGENCE SUMMARY.
(Erase heading not required.)

(Vol. 32)

Instructions regarding War Diaries and Intelligence Summaries are contained in F. S. Regs., Part II. and the Staff Manual respectively. Title pages will be prepared in manuscript.

Place	Date	Hour	Summary of Events and Information	Remarks and references to Appendices
BAVIN COURT	12/8		Took over D.A.D.V.S. office while on leave. DTR	
"	13		Nothing to report. DTR	
"	14		" " " DTR	
"	15		" " " DTR	
"	16		" " " DTR	
"	17		Prepared to move DTR	
"	18		Orders came to move 4 a.m. next morning DTR	
"	19		Entrained at MONDICOURT. DTR	
BAMBECQUE	20		Opened office at BAMBECQUE DTR	
"	21		Nothing to report. DTR	
"	22		" " " DTR	
"	23		" " " DTR	
"	24		Met A.D.V.S. II Corps DTR	
"	25		Nothing to report. DTR	
"	26		" " " DTR	
"	27		" " " DTR	

WAR DIARY
or
INTELLIGENCE SUMMARY.

Army Form C. 2118.

Place	Date	Hour	Summary of Events and Information	Remarks and references to Appendices
	28"		In office. T. R-m	
	29"		Set to no 2 V.E.S. II Corps. Inspected M.V.S. T. R-m.	
	30"		I went to No 2 V.E.S. & went with A.D.V.S. into inspected the ammunition 96th Inf. Brig. & M. Gun Battalion & 42 M.V.S. T. R-m.	
	31"		I attended horse in D.H.Q. T. R-m.	

Army Form C. 2118.

WAR DIARY
or
INTELLIGENCE SUMMARY.
(Erase heading not required.)

Confidential

War Diary
of
D.A.D.V.S. 32nd Division
From Aug 1st to Aug 31st 1918.
(Volume 33.)

G. Rees Mogg
MAJOR
D.A.D.V.S.
32nd DIVISION.

Army Form C. 2118.

WAR DIARY

~~INTELLIGENCE~~ SUMMARY

(Erase heading not required.)

D.A.D.V.S. 32nd Div.

Vol. 33

Number of pages 7.

Place	Date	Hour	Summary of Events and Information	Remarks and references to Appendices
DAM BECOURT	Aug 1		Went round all the 97th Inf. Brig. 92nd Field Amb & 219th Co. R.E. with the A.V.C. Sergt. Saw the A.D.C. 97th Brig. T.R-m.	
	2		Went round the 14th Inf Brig & 90th Field Amb north the Staff Captain	
	3		Inspected 42 M.V.S. I went to see the A.D.V.S. II Corps T. R-m	
	4		Saw the animals A.C. M.G. Batn on road & the staff of their Brig with & Wilson A.V.C. Anniversary Services held. T.R-m.	
	5		Inspected Capt ANDERSON V.O & C R.a & him the A.D.V.S. asph from D.H.Q. moved by train T.R-m.	
	6		Arrived station at FREYNCOURT at 5p.m arrived at new DHQ at 10½ p.m. T.R-m.	
	7		Advanced D.H.Q moved. Went to see Dentist. T.R-m.	
CAVILLON	8		Inspected 42 M.V.S. T.R-m	
	9		Rear A.D.V.S. moved to CAGNY. I tried to get car to go to advanced HQ at LE QUESNEL	
	10		I could not get one T.R-m	
	11		A.D.V.S. moved to BEAUCOURT. Went to advanced D.H.Q by M.L. 175 kilometres. Saw gun pumping & some shells of the much Tanks some killed by bombs & some	
CAGNY	12		lying dead on the 1st line area 88 & inspected retreat to HQ also Co. 32nd Div train Horses out of sight. Tan Office T.R-m	

Army Form C. 2118.

WAR DIARY
or
INTELLIGENCE SUMMARY.
(Erase heading not required.)

of D. A. D. V. S.
32 W Div

Place	Date	Hour	Summary of Events and Information	Remarks and references to Appendices
CAGNY	13		Adv. D.H.Q. returned to CAGNY. 32/32 V.S. moved to DOMART. 7 C.R.M.	
	14		I rode from 9.30 a.m. He Bt. m. I went to D.V.S. 14th Div. "99" Bryg. Byrg. & came both the Brigadiers - Staff Captains of the 16th & 7th Bryg. I received a memo. from a D.V.S. re Capt. REED Dis Barn & as Capt. REED had about the same questions to ask, he was acting for me & had sent the answered forms questions in the afternoon by motor to the I took them directly to the a D.V.S. Corps saying who my officers were. The day he wrote it was Capt. REED had returned from leave & the writer were implement & not done paid some things in his letter which were implement & not due. I sent the whole correspondence to the a.a. & D.M.S. of the 2nd Army then all the facts of the case were copied. He was done meanwhile under orders of the J.O.C. The a.a. & D.M.S. directed me to turn Capt. REED a.v.c. at D.H.Q. office at 8 a.m. 15th in the following day. J.R.M.	
	15		a.D.V.S. Canadian Corps came to see me. Inspected D.H.Q. Horses & Signal Co. horses. The J.O.C. interviewed Capt Dr. REED a.v.c. & told him that his motors direct to the staff or to the day that the D a.D.V.S. had returned was more irregular & that the contents of his letter was improper & untrue. Inspected J.R.m.	
	16		D.R. extra horses. Inspected 90th Field Amb. Horses. C R.M.	
	17		I went to see 96th Inf. Bry. I attended stud pick animals on D.H.Q. C.R.M.	

WAR DIARY
INTELLIGENCE SUMMARY

Army Form C. 2118.

D.A.D.V.S. 32nd Div.

Place	Date	Hour	Summary of Events and Information	Remarks and references to Appendices
	18		Went to take over from D.A.D.V.S. Aust Div at the new D.H.Q. Inspected the animals in Signal Coy. 5 P.M.	
	19		D.H.Q. moved to VILLERS BRETTONEUX. Went to see A.D.V.S. Corps. Inspected M.V.S. & Coy SMITH & Lt WILSON A.V.C. 5 R.M.	
VILLERS BRETTONEUX	20		Went to pay H.Q. Coy. & inspect & found Regtd off. Inspected M.V.S. from	
	21		Went to see Capt ANDERSON A.V.C. & saw the animals a 16-8. 3 P.M.	
	22		Inf. Brig at 12.19. 18-8. E. 5 R.M. Went to see A.D.V.S. AUSTRALIAN Corps & Lt NELSON 92 W Fell Ambulance. 5 R.M.	
	23		Nothing to report. 5 R.M.	
	24		Rev. H.Q. Inspected "Horse" Inspected the animals of 96 & 97 Bde Bty & 161st Bde S. Bombardment at 5 9.45 R.M. 3 officers & 3 ORs at Q. Loss. Rather damaged this neither my clerk & myself were injured. My clerks & I proceeded to Advance dressing Stn. 9 P.M. Took over & N. WILSON A.V.C. came to give me I attended to the wounded horses of 96 H.Q. Inf. Brig. Transport. 5 P.M.	
BAYON VILLERS	25		Inspected animals in 14th Inf. Brig. Transport. 5 P.M.	
	26		Went to see No 2 Section D.A.C. 89, Shell burst a met Capt J.SMITH A.V.C. Staff Sergt, went to see Capt W ANDERSON found the horses in 2 Batteries 168 Bry. R. F. A. in addition. Back at 7-30 P.M. I found a note awaiting me from	

WAR DIARY
INTELLIGENCE SUMMARY
(Erase heading not required.)

Army Form C. 2118.

D.A.D.V.S. 32 W Div.

Place	Date	Hour	Summary of Events and Information	Remarks and references to Appendices
	26(1/20)		He a a a Q.M.G. directing me to go over him at his office, him at 5-30 p.m. 23 Jan not return to my office till 7-30 p.m. I could not get off to be a A.Q.M.G.'s office till 7-35. The A & Q.M.G. was out but the G.S.O.2 who called me came to hut & wanted to know for me the open papers Rainbow had. I saw my letter referring to that I have a copy of this orders which he would not allow although was to him it I had orders not to double. The Mr. the order orders were kninded of viz. the letter last note to double. The A.O.C. appeared more writer by me on the 23rd inst. In my letter to him he Q.M.G. demo no. 1/1/M.G./8 dated D.A.D.V.S. land glad in about him a copy of the Q.Y.S. demo no. 1/1/11/8 in both of which he D.V.S. had glad a copy. Demo no. 30/11/8 dated 10/11/8 in both of which was that I recommend in horses going to the forage places did to relieve horses that I should go should be be bringing forage to harass the hay ration. I pointed out to take a of having the horses from D.Y.S.'s used monthly. I get off the necessary permission of horses in the hay ration. Before the second comment within the Moreage arrange he horses must have been considerable. Under these circumstances my letter & begged to recommend that D.R.O. be published at once canceling all the previous orders about bringing the chains to the other field next of the Rainers as I considered that as order therefore had now recommended - it was even ordinarily moving few major lines prevented the making commit things purtimentarily? D.led, these & long have. He Corps horses farmer that a the time deadline this morning chain all would be moved with

Army Form C. 2118.

WAR DIARY
or
INTELLIGENCE SUMMARY.
(Erase heading not required.)

D.A.D.V.S. 32nd Div.

Instructions regarding War Diaries and Intelligence Summaries are contained in F. S. Regs., Part II. and the Staff Manual respectively. Title pages will be prepared in manuscript.

Place	Date	Hour	Summary of Events and Information	Remarks and references to Appendices
			Reported that on journey to 97th Bde the animals knocked up & his turn-out that he could not enlist & that he the enemy had fully fouled trees & forty flak on land and getting a bit unless the animals not be unsafe on journey was shown. I asked the witness during the conversation how the animals at anything to how I relieved & the answer was 3 lbs hay 3 lbs oats. The witness had a similar tale to tell as the previous one although the animals did not appear the worse unfed. During the 3 line of 173 of Dec 20 31 Dec 33 animals have been provided for 31st & will during the list of 2 months a similar change always of for over not less than 23 animals were evacuated for mange. Showed but kind he only weighing range being the amount to a pile of no doubt in consequence of thorough & frequent grooming could not be carried out mainly owing to it being difficult to keep the animals warm. I ended up my letter as follows — "If my suggestion re the cancelling of the order re the trimming of sheep and head stock is carried out I am quite sure that in no little a "Turn out to the trenches." Hardly can go into a Transport line without hearing a Driver moaning "sick about trying to trim his his claws" B.R.M	

(A7092) Wt. W12839/M1295 752,000. 1/17. D. D. & L. Ltd. Forms/C.2118/14.

… A.D.V.S.
3-2 Dec

WAR DIARY
or
INTELLIGENCE SUMMARY.
(Erase heading not required.)

Place	Date	Hour	Summary of Events and Information	Remarks and references to Appendices
	27		The A.A. & Q.M.G. sent for me & told me that he had telephoned my letter to the G.O.C & that the S.O.S. was very annoyed & picked it up. the A.D.M.S. informed me that he had told the S.O.C. that he was sure that I had acted up for the benefit of the animals & that I was frankly badly worded for the transport of the left & that my Red would not take up offices. Drummond wrote a request to the A.A.S. on putting him forward my application to higher authority. Another Corps asking him to transferred away from this Division as from so possible consider the present circumstances. I was impossible for me to perform my duties & this with satisfaction to myself or as a credit to the Army Veterinary Corps. & I enclosed to the A.D.V.S. a copy of the whole correspondence connected with the matter. I turned out in my cabin the afternoon that I could have been funking on my duties as detailed in Chapter X. H. & II. of Field Service Regt. Part II & Veterinary Manual (25nd) 1915. Para. I.I. II. & II. 17. I had not done so to strict duty per A.D.V.S. 10. 9 so "everything in my power by recommendations to stop & prevent" "unnecessary wastage of horses especially there due to preventible diseases such as debility & mange, chapter 1. Para 1. & Kg Manual (2nd) 1915.	

T.R.M. |

Army Form C. 2118.

WAR DIARY
or
INTELLIGENCE SUMMARY.
(Erase heading not required.)

D.A.D.V.S. 32nd Div.

Place	Date	Hour	Summary of Events and Information	Remarks and references to Appendices
	28		Joined the MMVS behind the 2 x O.R.S. Gave the 32nd MVS orders him to unusual adequate shelter horses at niche. J. R-m.	
	29		Worked at side or D.H.Q. Went to see the A.D.V.S. moved. J. R-m.	
	30		M.V.S. I visited the wounded animals at D.H.Q. 32nd Field Amb. Received from Q a copy of a wire from the Q.M.G. re following "Hope Divisions make it impossible to evacuate horses and so frames of necessitated perigent orders being issued by you to ensure horses, vehicles of all kinds are not overloaded. Straggly, baggage also must be left behind under guard until they can be brought forward by rail or lorry. Blown on from aircraft is carefully considered." (Sd Aspl. Dir) J. R-m. The D.A.D.V.S. called for me & took me in his Car to the MDVS & opened at the Corps J. R-m.	

Army Form C. 2118.

WAR DIARY
or
INTELLIGENCE SUMMARY.
(Erase heading not required.)

Vol 34

Confidential

War Diary
of
D.A.D.V.S. 32nd Division
From 1st to 30th Sept. 1918.
(Volume 34).

G. Rootbigg
MAJOR
D.A.D.V.S.
32nd DIVISION.

Army Form C. 2118.

WAR DIARY
or
INTELLIGENCE SUMMARY.
(Erase heading not required.)

Place	Date	Hour	Summary of Events and Information	Remarks and references to Appendices

WAR DIARY

Army Form C. 2118.

A.A. & Q.M.G. 32nd Division

Vol. 34 (cont)

Place	Date	Hour	Summary of Events and Information	Remarks and references to Appendices
	5		The animals to be clearly seen are in good fettle. This has already occurred to the Quarmaster. I have not heard that any action was taken on my recommendation that the three weeks return to the A.D.M.S. should contain a written report on the wastage & as to whether the many units which were far away had no reply to my memo to R-m.	
	6		To M. Jan. Battn. Transport. Idid not get back till 9.30 p.m. I heard that the D.A.D.V.S. & A.D.V.S. were looking to see T.R-m. A.D.V.S. rushed me to go & see him at 2. I must have told him the D.V.S. had given him a letter from the D.V.S. hope an answer to my request that I might be transferred away from the Div. away to the G.O.C. electing to act contrary to my recommendations but that the D.V.S. did not see the way to do anything. T.R-m.	
	7			
	8		Rear D H.Q. moved Guinchecourt M.R.S. T.R.m.	
MISERY	9		Inspected 168 Bde R.F.A. 14th Inf Bde & Co. M. Gun Bath—T.R-m.	
"	10		Sent to see the M.P.S. lorry men & 16 animals from the various Units for evacuation. T.R-m.	
"	11		Ifook the weekly Returns to the AA & QMG. The AA & QMG told me that I had done wrong in sending my request to be transferred from the Div. thro' infantry channels. Don't think the Deputy Ginferred Him had I did not agree that it was purely a departmental affair. That the Great Channel was thro' the A.D.V.S. & Corps. To AA & QMG	

WAR DIARY
INTELLIGENCE SUMMARY

Army Form C. 2118.

D.A.D.M.S. 32nd Division

Vol. 34/(102)

Place	Date	Hour	Summary of Events and Information	Remarks and references to Appendices
	11		[illegible handwritten entries]	
	12			
	13			

WAR DIARY
or
INTELLIGENCE SUMMARY.
(Erase heading not required.)

Army Form C. 2118.

A.D.M.S. 32nd Div.

Vol 34 (cont.)

Place	Date	Hour	Summary of Events and Information	Remarks and references to Appendices
FOUILLOY	15th		10½ Visited the night Infans. D.H.Q. moved present to see A.C. 1½ Corps H.E.S. T.R.m. D.D.M.S. warned me by phone that when he showed me the D.M.S. reply to his note that A.D.M.S. to you was informed it to a fresh division as the G.O.C. felt sure that there must be some misunderstanding as though his remark the Division required was formed that he would be very sorry to withdraw me as the A.D.M.S. advice resulted to let this go altogether. I was thought to to have Junction R-m	
	16th		I went round the remainder of units they being A.D.M.S. of Bn. Boyen visited the Div. Sup. Brig. G.Rm.	
	17th		Inspected the M.K.S. of 97 S. Inf. Brig. T.R.M	
	18th		Worked in all day in case the A.D.M.S. might come	
	19th		Sgt MILLS R.A.M.C. attacked 96 inf Brig got the N.m head T.R.m. Junction see a Lieut. in 15 Lanc Fusiliers suspected Typhoid. T.M.K.S. T.R.m. L SUTHERLAND L M.K.S. T.R.m.	

Army Form C. 2118.

WAR DIARY
or
INTELLIGENCE SUMMARY.
(Erase heading not required.)

Vol. 3 A (con)   D.A.D.V.S. 3 2 W Dn

Place	Date	Hour	Summary of Events and Information	Remarks and references to Appendices
CORBIE	20/7		Took over from D.A.D.V.S. who proceed on leave, holding Divigord D.V.K.	
	21		Attended officers meeting of Divigord D.V.K.	
	22		" " "	
	23		Prepared to move D.V.K.	
BOUVIN COURT	24"		Divign office to BOUVINCOURT. D.V.K.	
	25		notify to Divgord D.V.K.	
	26		R.A.2.M.G. and Divign trace about shortage of remounts in trib wkly on	
	27/8		Received report to A.G. & 2.M.G. reported artlly anyone D.V.K	
	28/8		notify to Divgord D.V.K.	
	29"		D.A.D.V.S. returned from leave, enter D.V.K	
	30"		Inspected m.V.S. F.R.m	

Army Form C. 2118.

WAR DIARY
or
INTELLIGENCE SUMMARY.
(Erase heading not required.)

Confidential

War Diary
of
D.A.D.V.S. 32nd Division
From Oct. 1st to 31st 1918.
(Volume 35)

Maur Capt. AVC
A.D.V.S.
32nd Division

Army Form C. 2118.

WAR DIARY of J. a. D. V. S. 32nd Div.
INTELLIGENCE SUMMARY
(Erase heading not required.)

Vol. 35

Instructions regarding War Diaries and Intelligence Summaries are contained in F.S. Regs., Part II. and the Staff Manual respectively. Title pages will be prepared in manuscript.

Place	Date	Hour	Summary of Events and Information	Remarks and references to Appendices
BOUVINCOURT	Oct 1		Went to see A. WILSON a.v.c. but found that he had been evacuated from the C.C.S. to the base. So I went on to the A.D.V.S's office & informed the A.D.V.S. J.R-m.	
	2		I gave over to Capt. D.K. REED A.R.C. & go on with the M.Gun Battalion and Lt. WILSONS work. I took over the M.V.S. from Capt REED J R-m	
	3		Went to see the A.D.V.S. J.R-m	
	4		Visited Units in the forward area J R-m	
	5		Visited M.V.S. J R-m	
	6		I attended Conference J R-m	
	7		Rear D.H.Q. moved to P.K-m. Visited M.V.S. Visited Units in forward area. I spoke to the A.a.d.D.M.S. instructed me that the correspondence re Capt REED's leave had somewhat & had Maj O.C. No.1 mun Btn a long letter on the subject of the importance of some one absolutely attending the A. & Q.M. to write up correspondence. J R-m	
CATELET	8		Visited the M.V.S. & went home the O.C. V.E.S. J R-m	
	9		Visited Capt TIMONEY A.V.C. arrived & shook hands with him to the M.G. Battn J R-m	
	10		Saw Capt TIMONEY round the 14th 96th 97th Inf. Bde.	
	11		Visited the M.V.S. J R-m Visited the S.A. Section M.V.S. J R-m	

… WAR DIARY

OF

INTELLIGENCE SUMMARY.

D.A.D.V.S.
32nd Div.

Vol 35 (ten)

Place	Date	Hour	Summary of Events and Information	Remarks and references to Appendices
	12		Attended Conference at Corps. F.R-m.	
	13		Went to see Capt. REED at 41 Stationery Hosp. & found he had had leg off.	
	14		Demobilising duty. F.R-m	
	15		Inspecting Int Units F.R-m	
			Looked for Col to give me the RA but could not get one. Capt PAUL A.V.C. arrived. F.R-m	
	16		Saw Capt. PAUL A.V.C. & the D.A.C. Inspected m.v.S. F.R-m	
	17		Inspection Car to m.v.S. Capt. the R.A. F.R-m.	
	18		Inspected m.v.S. & passed the Int Transports in the morn F.R-m.	
	19		Took returns to A.D.V.S. arrived to m.v.S. F.R-m.	
	20		D.H.Q. moved to ...	
BOHAIN	21		Inspected m.v.S. & Transport. Went to see the 9 cases of Ice-Bourning in A. Coy 768 Lombd S.S. return & saw 2 to more. F.R-m.	
Busigny	22		I handed over to Capt PAUL A.v.c. & left for Corps. F.R-m.	
	23		Attended Office & visited units	
	24		do	
	25		do	
	26		do	
	27		do	
	28		do	while we moved to Busigny
	29		do	
	30		do	

Army Form C. 2118.

WAR DIARY
or
INTELLIGENCE SUMMARY.

(Erase heading not required.)

Instructions regarding War Diaries and Intelligence Summaries are contained in F.S. Regs., Part II. and the Staff Manual respectively. Title pages will be prepared in manuscript.

Place	Date	Hour	Summary of Events and Information	Remarks and references to Appendices
			Confidential War Diary of D.A.D.V.S. 32nd Division (Volume 20) for 30 November 1918	Vol 37

Army Form C. 2118.

WAR DIARY
or
INTELLIGENCE SUMMARY.
(Erase heading not required.)

Army S
32nd Division

(Volume 36)

Instructions regarding War Diaries and Intelligence Summaries are contained in F. S. Regs., Part II. and the Staff Manual respectively. Title pages will be prepared in manscript.

Place	Date	Hour	Summary of Events and Information	Remarks and references to Appendices
BUSIGNY	Nov 1		Attended Office. visited 16 F.S. & I.A.C. Maul	
	2		Took on Weekly Return to A.A. & Q.M.G. Visits Units & No 1 V.S. Maure	
	3		Attended Office. Visited Units & No. V.S. Maure	
	4		do do	
	5		do do	
	6		Office moved to BAZUEL also 42 M.V.S. Capt ANDERSON, V.C. 4 Artillery returned from leave	
BAZUEL	7		Attended Office in morning. Office moved in afternoon to FAVRIL Capt. REED A.V.C returned from Quettby took over charge of M.V.S.	
FAVRIL	8		Attended Office & visited I.A.C. & other units.	
	9		Office moved to GD FAYT. A.A. & I of Corps called Coinery Held Evacuation of Sick Guests Mickey Returned	
GD FAYT	10		Attended Office visited Units M.V.S. moved to PRISCHES	
	11		do M.V.S. moved to LES FOSSETTE	
	12		Office moved to AVESNES	
AVESNES	13		Attended Office visited Units	
	14		Office moved to SAINS DU NORD	
SAINS DU NORD	15		Attended Office visited Units	

Army Form C. 2118.

Instructions regarding War Diaries and Intelligence Summaries are contained in F. S. Regs., Part II. and the Staff Manual respectively. Title pages will be prepared in manuscript.

WAR DIARY
or
INTELLIGENCE SUMMARY.
(Erase heading not required.)

D.A.D.V.S. 32nd Division

(Volume 36).

Place	Date	Hour	Summary of Events and Information	Remarks and references to Appendices
SAINS 2d NORDJeole	16		M.V.S. moved to SAINS DU NORD. Went with Capt TIMONEY A.V.C. to RAMOUSIES. Investigated report that three horses had been cast as Veterinary Hospital for contagious disease. Reported to D.G. recommending two horses suspect "Off of Forage". Attended Officers' weekly visits.	
	17		do	
	18		do	
	19		Officers 9-11 A.S. moved to SIVRY.	
SIVRY	20		Officers 9-11. V.S. moved to RANCE. 42. M.V.S. went on to FOUR BECHIES.	
RANCE	21		Reported to A.A. & Q.M.G. Shot dead one horse with glanders in 100th BEGHIES area. Had notice Baths made good, hot tat & forms in their area. Attended Officers' weekly visits.	
	22		do	
	23		do	
	24		do	
	25		16. V.S. moved to CERFONTAINE. Reported to "Q" that post lubicult showers finished at CERFONTAINE.	
	26		Visited Units. Attended Officers' weekly visits daily.	
	27		do	
	28		do	
	29		do	
	30		do	

WAR DIARY

or
INTELLIGENCE SUMMARY.
(Erase heading not required.)

Army Form C. 2118.

L. a D. V. S.
32nd Division

Vol 3

Place	Date	Hour	Summary of Events and Information	Remarks and references to Appendices
B.O.L.	Aug 13		Received orders from 9 Corps to R.m.	
	14		Offices all day to R.m	
	15		Gave instructions for 2nd days march this & went to 9th F.E.S. to R.m	
	16		Office all day to R.m	
	17		Called P.o.a Buire to R.m	
	18		Gave lecture to 36 Bgde a.s.c. to R.m	
	19		Gave 2nd lecture to 3 BGde 160th Bgde to R.m	
	20		Gave 3rd lecture to Stands Sams & D to R.m	
	21		Saw Sick animals on Stands and E.D. to R.m	
	22		Saw some of the 97th Bgde Bivo to R.m	
	23		Went over the 97 & Ambulance & saw from 90 Fld Amb	
	24		Went Round the 96 from Boise to R.m	
	25		To the Mille wel 6th Ant ? & to be able to report to R.m	
	26		Went round a Farm in 62 A.S.C. Rode with the Apve Interest	
	27		Morrin R.C. Hosp to R.m	
	28		Antions A.C/m to R.m	
	29		Went to Mohil to inspect the day worth them with S.O. HAMERSLY Sere to R.m	
	30		Office all day to R.m	
	31		Meeting August to R.m	
			Summary Dec to R.m	

Will Carr RAVE
for Thos Clegg Cripol
D.A.D.V.S.
32nd Division

LANCASHIRE DIVISION
(LATE 32ND DIVN)

D.A.D.V.S
Ja - Nov.

D.A.DIR. VETY SERV.
JAN - ~~NOV 1915~~ DEC

WAR DIARY
or
INTELLIGENCE SUMMARY.
(Erase heading not required.)

Army Form C. 2118.

Confidential.

War Diary
of
D.A.D.V.S. 32nd Division
From Jan'y 1st to 31st 1919.
(Volume 38).

G. Rees Mogg
Major
D.A.D.V.S.
32nd Division.

Army Form C. 2118.

WAR DIARY
or
INTELLIGENCE SUMMARY.
(Erase heading not required.)

D.A.D.V.S. 32nd Divn.

Vol. 38

Place	Date 1919	Hour	Summary of Events and Information	Remarks and references to Appendices
BIOUL	JANY 1		Attended Office. Revised Nominal of S.H.Q. & Signals 9p	
	2		do 9p	
	3		do 9p made out Weekly Returns 9p	
	4		do visited Div H.Q. Signals Animals 9p	
	5		do 9p	
	6		do 9p	
	7		Commenced work of Veterinary Classifying Board. Classified animals 9p of 16.S Bde R.F.A. Attended Office at night	
	8		Cont. one day with Veterinary Classifying Board. Classified animals 9p of 16.1 Bde R.F.A	
	9		Classified animals of S.A.C. 9p	
	10		do do Divnl Train Office after tea 9p	
	11		do do Honour Battalion 9p	
	12		do of Machine Gun Bns 9p	
	13		do of 96th Bde Group 9p	

WAR DIARY
or
INTELLIGENCE SUMMARY.
(Erase heading not required.)

Army Form C. 2118.

Place	Date	Hour	Summary of Events and Information	Remarks and references to Appendices
BIOUL	1919 JANY 14		Classified arrivals of 14th Bde. Group. Attended Office after ten fro	
	15		do of 97th Bde. Group. do	
	16		do of 97th H. Qrs & returned Signals do	
	17		Attended Office. Sent off Weekly Returns	
	18		Attended Office in morning	
	19		Attended Office. arrival Units of D.A.C.	
	20		Visited Units of D.A.C. attended Office	
	21		do do	
	22		do do	
	23		At Office. visited M.I. Section	
	24		Attended Office. sent off Weekly Returns	
	25		do do Mobile Units.	
	26		do do	
	27		Visited the 4.5 do 9 Irregular arrivals of D.A a bateries D.A.C. W	
	28		Visited Units of D.A.T. D.A.C.	
	29		Welcome Anglais & Office 11 a.m.	
	30		Returned from In Office from	
	31		Office all day. 6 a.m.	

Army Form C. 2118.

WAR DIARY
or
~~INTELLIGENCE SUMMARY~~
(Erase heading not required.)

Vol. 39

Place	Date	Hour	Summary of Events and Information	Remarks and references to Appendices

D.A.D.V.S. 32nd Division

Confidential

War Diary

of

D.A.D.V.S. 32nd Division

From 1st to 28th February 1919.

(Volume 39)

J. Ramsay
Major
D.A.D.V.S.
32nd Division

WAR DIARY or INTELLIGENCE SUMMARY

Army Form C. 2118.

A.D.V.S. 32nd Div.

Vol. 39

(Erase heading not required.)

Instructions regarding War Diaries and Intelligence Summaries are contained in F.S. Regs., Part II. and the Staff Manual respectively. Title pages will be prepared in manuscript.

Place	Date	Hour	Summary of Events and Information	Remarks and references to Appendices
BLOL	July 1		In office all morning. Left at 2 p.m. for NAMUR en route for G.H.Q.	
BOYNE	2		Arrived at 2 p.m. Went to see A.D.V.S. at G.H.Q.	
	3		Went to see A.D.R.S. G.R.m.	
	4		Went to see Capt. ANDERSON & Staff Captain R.A. G.R.m.	
	5		Had a D.R.O. put in re the clipping of the heads necks & withers of all horses as a means to diagnosing any cases of Mange in the early stage.	
	6		Went to VILICH to find billets for the M.V.S. G.R.m. Went to see horses in 158th Bde. in morning & went to M.V.S. at the station at 3 p.m. on their arrival. G.R.m.	
	7		Went to Capt. ANDERSON A.V.C. & see Z/Hop/61 re Brig Gen Jefferson to see general civilian horses reported to be suffering from Glanders but the disease turned out to be Mange G.R.m. & 97th Inf. Brig. Hd Qrs. G.R.m.	
	8		Went to see the new Z/161 & 97th Inf. Brig. Hd Qrs. G.R.m.	
	9		Conference of T.O. & Staff of Corps Remount Bont interviewed Mallein a few horses in D.H.Q.	
	10		Forwarded (Capt D.V. REEDS) application to proceed in Army of Occupation & I recommended that he be sent for a tour of duty at a Base G.G. Hospital G.R.m.	
	11		Inspected his horse gass D. to attend in morn. at 2-30 attended the Remount Board & inspected horses in Manchesters 218th D.A.S. & to 3rd C. Div. Train G.R.m.	
	12		Office all day. G.R.m.	
	13		Went round the horses in 96th Inf. Brig. G.R.m.	
	14		Went to place one gathering & also 8 animals & men on to see the Corps Horse Adviser. G.R.m.	

Army Form C. 2118.

WAR DIARY
or
INTELLIGENCE SUMMARY.
(Erase heading not required.)

D.A.D.V.S. 32nd Div.

Vol. 39.

Instructions regarding War Diaries and Intelligence Summaries are contained in F.S. Regs., Part II. and the Staff Manual respectively. Title pages will be prepared in manuscript.

Place	Date	Hour	Summary of Events and Information	Remarks and references to Appendices
BONN	Feb 15		Went to see the Corps Horse Adviser on A.D.V.S. F.R.M.	
	16		V.O. came to see me. In office F.R.M.	
	17		Gutlebem Caturkh. H.O. 1/5. 14th Lgt Inf. Brigades to see M.R.S. 97th Inf Bgd. in morning. Saw off 2 Offs. in gun Batt. 219 & R. & 97 Lt H. Arty.	
	18		Went with D.A.D.S. to try hand Clipping machine Horses of 97th D Inf. visited the Royal Scots & 15th H.L.I. Brigade transport F.R.M.	
	19		Attended Conference at Corps re grazing of Manage amongst the German civilian horses & discussed amongst other matters D.A.D.V.S. F.R.M.	
	20		In office attending sick animals. Wrote in a few recommendations	
	21		Inspected Bgde H.O. of the m.m.g Squadron. F.R.M.	
	22		Went to M.R.S. Inspected wiring supplies to questions where Sanitation.	
	23		R.A.F. C. Organization in our Balloon Army. F.R.M.	
	24		In office continued my Rep. B.G. B.R.A. Art O. re the sale of the Horses of many tents to A.D.V.S. F.R.M.	
	25		Sent to see the Top. 2 Staff Captain R.O. to be the evacuation of the animals by V.S. F.R.M.	
	26		Compiled at 2 Inspected the animals for evacuation to M.V.S. F.R.M.	
	27		Went to see the animals in 15th & 16th Line Transport in main Lines & f 2 Guns to see the Abattoir at COLOGNE Rendered our animals arrival all right by train	
	28		Went to see A.D.V.S. Defective Horses. Inspection Committee letter to F.R.M. Organization to Scale. Attended Remount Board with the D.D.R. F.R.M.	

WAR DIARY
or
INTELLIGENCE SUMMARY.

(Vol. 40)

Confidential
War Diary
of
A. A. & Q.M.G. Lancashire Division.
From Mar 1st to 31st 1919.
(Volume 40).

G Rey Mogg
Major
A.A.&Q.M.G. Lancs. Division

WAR DIARY or INTELLIGENCE SUMMARY

(Erase heading not required.)

Army Form C. 2118.

D.A.D.V.S.
Lane
32nd Div.

Vol. 40

Place	Date	Hour	Summary of Events and Information	Remarks and references to Appendices
BONN	March 2		Inspected animals for evacuation at M.V.S. 9 R.m.	
	3		Inspected animals for the Pioneer Batt. & Signal Co. 5 R.m.	
	4		Inspected M.V.S. & D.V.S. at R.m.	
	5		D.V.S. at his inspection to M.V.S. & in apt. inspected a few units. 9 R.m.	
	6		Accompanied a D.D.V.S. to inspect Remount Board on reclassifying Z animals in the R.A. & Div. Train. 5 R.m.	
	7		Accompanied Remount Board on reclassifying Z animals at Collecting Camp. 1 at 11 attended A.D.V.S. Conference	
	8		Inspected 110 Z horses gave to see the new & animals arrive. 9 R.m.	
	9		Went to pay the a. D.V.S. marked to see the new & animals arrive. 9 R.m.	
			Nothing of import in office. 9 R.m.	
	10		Went to Col V to see pretty animals evacuated from	
	11		Inspected the animals in 13 Kink Rifle Regt & 15" & 16" Lane. Fus. 5 R.m.	
	12		Inspected the animals in Div. Signal Co. & went to see the a.D.V.S. 5 R.m.	
	13		Inspected the animals in Machine Gun Battalion. 5 R.m.	
	14		Accompanied Remount Board reclassifying Z animals in 161 & Brigt. 9 R.m.	
	15		Inspected M.V.S. 9 R.m.	
	16		Met new Divisional Commander. 5 R.m.	
			Inspected animals in Forests & D. Coy. M. Gun Batt" & went to the	
	17		M.V.S. at 5 p.m. I distributed 14.9 x animals just arrived. 9 R.m.	
	18		I accompanied Remount Board on reclassifying Z animals. I went to all Personally the Transport Officers of 15" & 16" Lane. Fus. & Signal Co. re pending Z animals away. 9 R.m.	

WAR DIARY or INTELLIGENCE SUMMARY

Army Form C. 2118.

D.A.D.V.S. Lanzf 32nd Div.

Vol. 40(c)

Place	Date	Hour	Summary of Events and Information	Remarks and references to Appendices
Bohain	19		Went to see 2 animals off & inspected the R.O. of L.L.S. animals of C. Coy M. Gun Battn. 5 P.M.	
	20		Inspected M.V.S. & sent in a written report for the use of a Car every morning. 5 P.M.	
	21		Distributed remounts & animals. 5 P.M.	
	22		Inspected 2 animals going away. 5 P.M.	
	23		Inspected 2 animals going away & 2 Remounts arriving at 18 o'clock 5 P.M.	
	24		The Veterinarian of the A.R.Q.M.G. of the said Rahts and allotted a Car 5 P.M.	
			Remounts & arranged a week. 5 P.M.	
	25		Inspected M.R.S. & field amb. & attended a Board on S. Smiths. 5 P.M.	
	26		Inspected M.R.S. Units 28 & 26 A.D.V.S. 5 P.M.	
	27		Inspected M.R.S. & found a bad shrew horse and gave it 5 P.M.	
	28		Inspected A.D.V.S. & Corps Officer & inspected 10 of C. Grand Inspected the Rem. C.O. 97 Inf Bng & arranged to give a lecture on animal management to his new Boys Battalions 5 P.M.	
	29		Inspected Remounts in 96 Inf Bng & gave lectures on animal management to the 96 Inf. Bng. & started the & at D.S. of 5 P.M.	
	30		Busy with Returns D.A.Q. 5 P.M.	
	31		Inspected the 57th Kings Liverpool Regt. I gave a lecture to the 15th 16th Kings June on animal Management. Went to the animal Collecting Camp Estn. & saw 2 animals entrained 5 P.M.	

Army Form C. 2118.

WAR DIARY
~~INTELLIGENCE SUMMARY.~~
(Erase heading not required.)

Instructions regarding War Diaries and Intelligence Summaries are contained in F. S. Regs., Part II. and the Staff Manual respectively. Title pages will be prepared in manuscript.

Place	Date	Hour	Summary of Events and Information	Remarks and references to Appendices

CONFIDENTIAL

WAR DIARY OF

D.A.D.V.S. LANCASHIRE DIVISION

FROM APRIL 1ST TO APRIL 30TH 1919.

(VOLUME 41.)

F C Syming Lieut. Cd.
D.A.D.V.S.
Lancs. Division

2nd Sheet

WAR DIARY
or
INTELLIGENCE SUMMARY

Army Form C. 2118.

D.A.D.V.S. Lancs. Div. XXII

Place	Date April	Hour	Summary of Events and Information	Remarks and references to Appendices
[Town]	21		Inspected animals of 3rd Lancs. Inf. Bde. with Capt. Timoney	T.O.
"	22		" of 1st Lancs Inf. Bde. with Lieut. Col. Knott & Capt. Timoney	T.O.
"	23		Lancs M.V.S. with Lieut. Col. Knott R.A.V.C. Inspected the animals of Div. Am. Sn.	T.O.
"	24		" animals of R.A. & D. Bty. of 32 Dn. M.G.C. also those of Hd. Qrs. 32 Dn. M.G.C.	T.O.
			War supply officer in reference to forage supplied for men (DAQMG to publish return on the subject)	
"	25		Examined a complete new mule of the new O.C. 1/8 Manchester Regt.	T.O.
			Inspected mules of C.R.A. Lancs Div.	
"	26		Reported at office of ADVS to attend at 9.30 a.m. Interviewed Staff Captain R.A. in certain of certain animals in R.A. Am. Sn. Went to Advanced Vet. Stores	T.O.
"	27		Hd. Qrs. Lancs Div. with returns	T.O.
"	28		Visited Lancs M.V.S. at Vilich	T.O.
"	29		Visited officer returns	T.O.
"	30		Inspected the animals of 1st Dn. Lancs. Div.	T.O.
			" D.A.C. with Lt. Col. Knott R.A.V.C.	
			" Lancs M.V.S.	

Army Form C. 2118.

WAR DIARY or INTELLIGENCE SUMMARY.

D.A.D.V.S.
Lancs ? Div
32nd Div
Vol II

Place	Date	Hour	Summary of Events and Information	Remarks and references to Appendices
BOMN	April 1		Went round the 16th Brig R.F.A. with A.D.V.S. & at 2 lectured on animal management to the 14th Inf Brig. Bde. R.F.A. 3 p.m.	
	2		Inspected animals 53rd Manchesters & lectured to them 3 p.m.	
	3		Went round the animals 168th Brig R.F.A. with the A.D.V.S. 6 p.m.	
	4		The Div. Commander paid a surprise visit to the M.S. & found everything in a filthy condition. Gave me a hour's relieve Capt REED of his charge at once & put Capt GORDON R.A.V.C. in charge.	
	5		Went to M.V.S. & gave a lecture to party of the 97th Inf. Reg. 3 p.m.	
	6		All V.O.s came to see me 3 p.m.	
	7		Went to see the A.D.V.S. Inspected horses and D.H.Q. 3 p.m.	
	8		Went round R.S. & 266th R.E. & gave advice Report by O.C. pr Capt. REED R.A.V.C. to sign 3 p.m.	
	9		Accompanied the Div Commander for inspection of D.A.C. 3 p.m. & reinforcements of R.A.M.C. 3 p.m.	
	10		Went to see D.V.S. re Remounts 3 p.m.	
	11		Went to see Remounts 3 p.m.	
	12		Went to see Remounts 3 p.m.	
	13		Office all day 3 p.m.	
	14		Went to M.S. & gave 2 P.Os 3 p.m.	
	15		Visits and inspected the Port Bellum remount train 3 p.m.	
	16		Went saw A.D.V.S. Major BORRIDGE animal and D.A.D.V.S. 3 p.m.	
	17		Took Col. Burridge round the 169th Brig R.F.A. 3 p.m.	
	18		Took Col. Burridge round the MV.S. & 168th Brig R.F.A. 3 p.m.	
	19		Took Col. Burridge round the D.A.C. & handed over him 3 p.m.	
	20		Comprise of the V.O's & Issued Ins. & officer of D.A.D.V.S. to D.	

Army Form C. 2118.

WAR DIARY
or
INTELLIGENCE SUMMARY.
(Erase heading not required.)

Confidential

War Diary

of

D.A.D.V.S. Lancashire Division

From May 1st to 31st 1919.

(Volume 42.)

F. Dunn Lieut Col
D.A.D.V.S. Lancs Division

Army Form C. 2118.

1st Shot

D.A.D.V.S.
Lancs Div

WAR DIARY
or
INTELLIGENCE SUMMARY.
(Erase heading not required.)

Instructions regarding War Diaries and Intelligence Summaries are contained in F. S. Regs., Part II. and the Staff Manual respectively. Title pages will be prepared in manuscript.

Place	Date	Hour	Summary of Events and Information	Remarks and references to Appendices
LONH	1.5.19		Visited Officers in/charge Supplies & reported on Culturn remounts received by 161st Div on their arrival in the station.	T.S.(1)
	2.5.19		Inspected animals of Al Bn 2nd Lancs. Div., 91st Field Ambulance, 1/5 Border Regt., 218 Coy R.E.	T.S.(2)
	3.5.19		Redemphied 100 surplus mules of D.A.C. & saw all the horses on trade of trips.	T.S.(3)
	4.5.19		Inspected animals of 10th & 11th Bns. Lancs. Fus.	T.S.(4)
	4.5.19		Read & wrote Lancs. Div. wkly mbl report. Inspected horses of Divisional Commander.	T.S.(5)
	5.5.19		Proceed to inspection of Lancs. M.V.S. & harness remounts. Reported to new ADVS I Corps (Col. TATE)	T.S.(6)
	6.5.19		Inspected & attended on certain animals for transfer at O/16K Div	T.S.(7)
			Letter to Officer i/c 325 M.G.C. Visited their section	
	7.5.19		Inspected MT & P. Horses at MYLDORP. BIGGSBURG & OBER. CASSEL MK DEPT.	T.S.(8)
	8.5.19		Inspected Lancs. M.V.S. & transport ADVS I Corps on visit of inspection to R.V.S.	T.S.(9)
	9.5.19		Conference & Maj G ADVS I Corps. Capt HOWARD RAVE return from leave	T.S.(10)
	10.5.19		Inspected head & horse animals & visited officers station	T.S.(11)
	11.5.19		Visited Administrative	T.S.(12)
	12.5.19		Inspected fld ambulance 1/166 DL R.F.A. visited Lancs. M.V.S.	T.S.(13)
	13.5.19		Inspected the stables of Lancs. Div. Signals	T.S.(14)
	14.5.19		Jupiter & horses of 2d. the Lancs. Div. & 4/12 B R.A. Lancs. Div. visited T.V.E.S. on trans to inspect surplus remounts for return to C.R. & surplus sig. of D.A.C. Lancs. Div. Capt METIVIER return from leave.	T.S.(15)
	15.5.19		Visited Lancs. Div. Arm. with ADVS I Corps. Saw Arm. remount (DEVER) reinquarters of patients.	T.S.(16)

D. D. & L., London, E.C.
(A12056) Wt.W300/P713 750,000 2/13 Sch. 52 Forms/C2118a.

WAR DIARY
or
INTELLIGENCE SUMMARY.

(Erase heading not required.)

Army Form C. 2118.

2nd Sheet

D.A.D.V.S. Lancs Divn

Instructions regarding War Diaries and Intelligence Summaries are contained in F.S. Regs., Part II. and the Staff Manual respectively. Title pages will be prepared in manuscript.

Place	Date	Hour	Summary of Events and Information	Remarks and references to Appendices
BONN	16.5.19		Visited Lancs Div M.V.S. Usual office routine	T.B.B
"	17.5.19		Inspection of horses with remounts. Capt Gorden R.A.V.C. left Lancs Div for England	T.B.B
"	18.5.19		Read duties Lancs Div. M.V.S. visited A.D.V.S. re arrangements with R.E. re erection of manger etc	T.B.B
"	19.5.19		Inspected animals of Mr & brig Genl train, 91st Field Amb, A.V. 2nd 2 Lancs Inf Bde	T.B.B
"			Saw ADVS re RE re repairs, whitewash + lub. heater in stables of 3rd Coy Divnl Train	T.B.B
"	20.5.19		Inspection animals of 161st Fd Amb - Inspected animals of 3rd Coy Divnl Train with A.D.V.S. I Corps	T.B.B
"	21.5.19		Inspection of animals A + B 2/c Lancs Div + A+B 2/c R.A. Lancs Div. Usual office routine	T.B.B
"	22.5.19		Inspection of 91st Fd Amb, A+B 2/c Lancs Inf Bde + C.Coy Div Train + B/161 Bde	T.B.B
"	23.5.19		Inspection of animals of 1/5 Border Regt, 91st Fd Amb, Div Supply + B/161 Bde	T.B.B
"	24.5.19		Visited Lancs Div M.V.S.	T.B.B
"	25.5.19		Inspected horses & stables of 15th + 16th Lancs Fus. Usual office routine	T.B.B
"	26.5.19		Usual routine	T.B.B
"	27.5.19		Went to office of C.R.E. about stable fittings + more stables. Saw A.D.V.S. regarding reports on same. Visited Lancs M.V.S. re inspection animals for remounts	T.B.B
"	28.5.19		Inspected animals of 51st, 62nd + 63rd Bty Manchester Regt	T.B.B
"			Inspection of animals of Hd, 2nd Lancs Div + Hd 2nd R.A. Lancs Div Capt Lavery reported for duty with Lancs Div from N. H. V. H., Rouen. Usual office routine	T.B.B
"	29.5.19		Inspected animals of Hd 2nd 94c + S.A.A. Sect. D.A.C. Lancs Div. Inspection 1/2 + bay Div Train in	T.B.B
"			conjunction with A.D.V.S. I Corps	T.B.B
"	30.5.19		Usual office routine. Capt Mortimer returned from leave	T.B.B
"	31.5.19		Inspection of Lancs M.V.S. by D.D.V.S. + A.D.V.S. I Corps	T.B.B

WAR DIARY
or
~~INTELLIGENCE SUMMARY~~

Army Form C. 2118.

Confidential

War Diary

D.A.D.V.S. Lancashire Division

From June 1st 1919 to 30th 1919.

(Volume 43)

A.E.W. Stone
Captain
for Lieut Col
D.A.D.V.S Lancashire Div.

1st Sheet   D.A.D.V.S.
             LANCS. DIV

Army Form C. 2118.

WAR DIARY
or
INTELLIGENCE SUMMARY.
(Erase heading not required.)

Instructions regarding War Diaries and Intelligence Summaries are contained in F.S. Regs., Part II. and the Staff Manual respectively. Title pages will be prepared in manuscript.

Place	Date	Hour	Summary of Events and Information	Remarks and references to Appendices
	1.6.19		Visit matters	To A
	2.6.19		Inspected animals & stables of No.1 & No.2 Sections D.A.C. LANCS DIV Inspection of LANCS M.V.S.	To B
	2.6.19		Inspection of animals of 13th Bn Kings Liverpool Regt. + 92nd Field Ambulance	To B
	4.6.19		Inspection of animals of HQ 2nd LANCS. DIV, HQ 2nd RA + CRE + LANCS DIV SIGNAL COY	To B
	5.6.19		Inspected details of 13th KINGS REGT + 51st + 52nd Bn. KINGS REGT.	To B
			Inspected sick animals of Hd. quarters of LANCS. M.V.S.	To B
	6.6.19		Visit Officer matters	To B
	7.6.19		Inspection of horses of 12th Bn L.N. LANCS (PIONEERS)	To B
	8.6.19		Visit matters	To B
	9.6.19		Visit matters	To B
	10.6.19		Inspection of No.1 Coy Divisional Train + HQ 2nd M.G.C. (32nd Div)	To B
	11.6.19		Inspection of some Infirmm had horses at stables Infirmm of many cases at IV.E.S.	To B
	12.6.19		Inspected animals of B. Coy 9. C (32nd Div) + 2/168 Bn	To B
			Inspection of animals of 219 Coy R.E. Report of A.D.V.S. Telegra Visits from M.V.S. + Infirm. sick animals of inspection	To B
	13.6.19		Visit Officer matters	To B
	14.6.19		Visit Officer of A.D.V.S. Inspected material of 206 Field Coy R.E.	To B
	15.6.19		Inspection of H.V.B. of LANCS. DIV	To B
	16.6.19		Office of A.D.V.S. Ty Ease Visit matters	To B
	17.6.19		Inspected stable + animals of D.A.C. LANCS DIV. HQ 2nd 2nd LANCS. INF. DIV + 91st Field Ambulance	To B
	18.6.19		Inspection of animals of HQ 2 LANCS DIV + RE + LN + 3rd LANCS. FUS.	To B
	19.6.19		Visit matters	To B

2nd Sheet

Army Form C. 2118.

WAR DIARY
or
INTELLIGENCE SUMMARY.
(Erase heading not required.)

D.A.D.V.S. Lancs. Div.

Instructions regarding War Diaries and Intelligence Summaries are contained in F.S. Regs., Part II. and the Staff Manual respectively. Title pages will be prepared in manuscript.

Place	Date	Hour	Summary of Events and Information	Remarks and references to Appendices
	20.6.19		Visit routine. Inspected LANCS. M.V.S. Afore moving fm VILICH to SIEGBERG RANGE	T.B.D
	21.6.19		Inspected A. bred sick animals. Visit office routine.	T.B.D*
	22.6.19		Visit routine.	T.B.D
	23.6.19		Inspection of Lancs. M.V.S. at Siegberg.	
	24.6.19		Visit routine; Lieut T.B. Banister R.A.V.C. proceeded on Pair leave; Capt H.V. Metherington o.i. M.V.S Lancs Div took over the duties of D.A.D.V.S	routine
	25.6.19		Usual office routine.	
	26.6.19		Sick animals on Nat.16 inspected. Office routine	routine to-wa
	27.6.19		Weekly returns — office routine as usual	
	28.6.19		Usual office routine.	routine
	29.6.19		Conference D.V.O.S. Visited A.D.V.S X Corps.	routine
	30.6.19		Inspection of animals on Lancs Div. Nat 16. Office routine	

HVW Hetherington Capt
act. D.A.D.V.S
Lancs. Division.

WAR DIARY
~~INTELLIGENCE SUMMARY~~
(Erase heading not required.)

Army Form C. 2118.

Confidential
War Diary
D.A.D.V.S. Lancashire Division
From July 1st 1919 to 31st 1919
(Volume 44)

J.A. Rowe
Major
D.A.D.V.S. Lancashire Division

Army Form C. 2118.

1st Sheet

WAR DIARY
or
INTELLIGENCE SUMMARY.
(Erase heading not required.)

D.A.D.V.S. Lancashire Division

Instructions regarding War Diaries and Intelligence Summaries are contained in F. S. Regs., Part II. and the Staff Manual respectively. Title pages will be prepared in manuscript.

Place	Date	Hour	Summary of Events and Information	Remarks and references to Appendices
Bouen	1-7-19		Grateful local sick horses: Office Routine as usual	HM
	2-7-19		Office routine: D.A.D.V.S returned from seven days Paris leave.	HM
	3-7-19		V.Os reported with their weekly Returns	HM
	4-7-19		Usual routine	To D
	5-7-19		Usual routine	To D
	6-7-19		Usual routine	To D
	7-7-19		Usual routine	To D
	8-7-19		CAPT. TIMONEY R.A.V.C. reported duration on leave to U.K	To D
	9-7-19		Inspection of animals of 161 Bde R.F.A. in company with A.D.V.S. X Corps	To D
	10-7-19		Inspection of animals of 1st & 2nd 166 Bde R.F.A	To D
	11-7-19		Usual office routine	To D
	12-7-19		Inspection of animals of LANCS. DIV. SIGNALS reported to A.A.2.M.G. in stables	To D
	13-7-19		Usual routine. Visited 42nd M.V.S. VILICH	To D
	14-7-19		Inspection of animals of "A" Bty 32nd M.G.C	To D
	15-7-19		Inspection of animals of 13th & 61st KINGS (LIVERPOOL) Regts.	To D
	16-7-19		Classification of animals Lancs D.A.C R.A.H. 2nd & 161st Bde	To D

A6945 Wt. W11422/M160 35,000 12/16 D. D. & L. Forms/C/2118/14.

2nd Sheet

Army Form C. 2118.

WAR DIARY
or
INTELLIGENCE SUMMARY.
(Erase heading not required.)

D.A.D.V.S. Lancashire Division

Instructions regarding War Diaries and Intelligence Summaries are contained in F. S. Regs., Part II. and the Staff Manual respectively. Title pages will be prepared in manuscript.

Place	Date	Hour	Summary of Events and Information	Remarks and references to Appendices
BOAN	17.7.19		Classification of animals of 206th 216th & 219th Coys R.E. & Lancs. Div. Train	To A
"	18.7.19		Classification of remounts of 166th Bde R.F.A., 52 Kings (Liverpool) Regt.	To A
"	19.7.19		Surveyed Whly	To A
"	20.7.19		Usual routine	To A
"	21.7.19		Classification of remounts of 5th Kings, 15th & 16th Lancs. Fus., 12 L.N. Lancs. & Div Signal Coy	To A
"	22.7.19		Classification of remounts of 3rd (Manchester) Bde. 91st & 92nd Field Ambulances	To A
"	23.7.19		Classification of remounts of 32nd M.G.C. 9 & 42 M.V.S. Capt Timoney returned from leave	To A
"	24.7.19		Usual routine	To A
"	25.7.19		Visit Major A.D.V.S. re Capes in departure to England	To A
"	26.7.19		Usual routine	To A
"	27.7.19		Usual routine	To A
"	28.7.19		Usual routine	To A
"	29.7.19		Major Bt. Lt. Col. T.E. Burridge R.A.V.C. proceeded to England on landing over the duties of D.A.V.S. Lancashire Division to Major Z.H.M. Thomas R.A.V.C who reported this arrival this day. Usual routine.	t.W.F.

3rd Sheet D.A.D.V.S. Lancashire Division

Army Form C. 2118.

WAR DIARY
or
INTELLIGENCE SUMMARY.
(Erase heading not required.)

Place	Date	Hour	Summary of Events and Information	Remarks and references to Appendices
Bov.	30.7.19		Moral routine. Visited 42nd M.V.S. Vital.	A.D.V.S.
"	31.7.19		Inspection of C.D.A.H3. Batteries 168th Brigade R.F.A. by A.D.V.S. Xth Corps	A.D.V.S.

WAR DIARY
~~INTELLIGENCE SUMMARY~~

Army Form C. 2118.

Confidential

War Diary

A.A.D.S. Lancashire Division

From Aug 1st to 31st 1919.

(Volume 45)

J.W. Crowe
Major.
D.A.D.O.S. Lancashire Div.

Army Form C. 2118.

1st sheet

WAR DIARY D.A.D.V.S. Lancashire Division
or
INTELLIGENCE SUMMARY.
(Erase heading not required.)

Place	Date	Hour	Summary of Events and Information	Remarks and references to Appendices
Bonn	1.8.19		Manal routine	J.D.V.S.
"	2.8.19		Interviewed Lt Friedman Govt Veterinary Inspector Bonn with ref to a suspected case of Glanders at a farm at Geislar. Round nothing	J.V.S.
"	3.8.19		Proceeded to Geislar. Inspected animal belonging to Heinrich Schmitz suspected of Glanders. The ponies on both sides of the road were cut out & hounds of all troops until further notice. Instructed Capt Webber to take a Pus smear from a lesion on the suspected animal in order to examine it microscopically for B. mallei lymphangitis.	
"	4.8.19		Visited M.V.S. Which was informed by O.C. M.V.S. that the C.R.E. Lancashire Division had visited the M.V.S. & was greatly pleased with all he saw. Captain T.M. Tinkey R.A.V.C. admitted to the Hospital suffering from gastritis. Sick horse from the civilian horse at Geislar inspected. 6 further animals taken.	
"	5-8-19		Classification of animals of horses of 6th Border Regiment	J.D.V.S.

2nd Sheet

Army Form C. 2118.

WAR DIARY
or
INTELLIGENCE SUMMARY.
(Erase heading not required.)

D.A.D.V.S. Lancashire Division

Place	Date	Hour	Summary of Events and Information	Remarks and references to Appendices
Bonn	5-8-19		At 2nd Bde H.Q. Capt: J.F. Lowry admitted to C.C.S. with appendicitis.	AWF
"	6-8-19		Inspection of horses of Lancashire Divisional H.Q. Swears taken from two civilian horse at Girwler confirmed as epizootic lymphangitis. Accompanied A.D.V.S. & Corps V.O. interviews Dr Tillemann Govt. Veterinary Inspector Bonn with ref to above case of epizootic lymphangitis.	AWF
"	7-8-19		Inspection of stables & horses of Lancashire Divnl H.Q. Proceeded with A.D.V.S. & Corps V.O. Tillemann Govt. Vety Surgeon Bonn to Girwler to inspect & arrange about the destruction of the animal suffering from epizootic lymphangitis belonging to Heinrich Schulz taken to hospital for the disinfection of the premises. Inspection of the horses of the 91st (Irish) Ambulance.	AWF
"	8-8-19		Visited H.Q. 1st Bde Col CP & 2nd Lt Col R.E. Pilcken visited 42 M.S. Field Stable in course of erection for this unit leaving completion.	AWF

3rd Sheet.

D.A.D.V.S. Lancashire Division

Army Form C. 2118.

WAR DIARY
or
INTELLIGENCE SUMMARY.
(Erase heading not required.)

Place	Date	Hour	Summary of Events and Information	Remarks and references to Appendices
Bonn	9.8.19		Visited Rondorf: arrival of Bwinal A.D.S. Arrived ready	$45
"	10.8.19		Manual routine	
"	11.8.19		Inspected animals at M.G.C. billeted in the remnt of Geislar. Capt. J.B. Little R.A.V.C. reported his arrival for duty in the Div.	$45
"	12.8.19		Classification of animals proceeding much - not clearly classified at Bonel & at Artillery Barracks Bleiendorf Strasse	$45
"	13.8.19		Accompanied A.D.V.S. X th Corps at his inspection of N° 14 Coy Div. Train & N° 2 Coy Div. Train. Also to Siegburg inspected there D? N° 1 & 3 Coys Large Div. Trains by A.D.V.S. X Corps.	$45
"	14.8.19			$45 $45
"	15.8.19		Manual routine	
"	16.8.19		Manual routine	
"	17.8.19		Manual routine. Proceeded to Siegburg with A.D.V.S. Corps to interview Dr Richter Govt Veter Surgeon Siegburg acting for Dr Guldeman Bonn, with reference to the destruction of the case of Zymotic Lymphangitis at Geislar village	

4th Sheet.
D.A.D.V.S. Lancashire Division

Army Form C. 2118.

WAR DIARY
or
INTELLIGENCE SUMMARY.
(Erase heading not required.)

Place	Date	Hour	Summary of Events and Information	Remarks and references to Appendices
Bonn	17.8.19 (cont)		He informed me that the animal had been destroyed and it was arranged that in future supervise the destruction of the premises at Geislar.	
"	18.8.19		Usual routine.	
"	19.8.19		Usual routine.	
"	20.8.19		Board on Shoeing Smith at D.A.C. Cavalry Barracks Bonn. Visited 42 M.V.S. Wich.	
"	21.8.19		Inspection of all civilian animals in the village of Geislar. No further suspicious cases of sporadic lymphangitis or other contagious disease was found. Visited animal at 52nd Machine Gun Regt at Mundorfen. Inspection of No. 42 M.V.S. by D.V.S. Army of the Rhine accompanied by the A.D.V.S. X Corps.	2W.S.
"	22.8.19		Usual routine.	2W.S.
"	23.8.19		Usual routine.	2W.S.
"	24.8.19		Usual routine.	2W.S.

Army Form C. 2118.

5th Sheet.
D.A.D.V.S. Lancashire Division

WAR DIARY
or
INTELLIGENCE SUMMARY.
(Erase heading not required.)

Instructions regarding War Diaries and Intelligence Summaries are contained in F. S. Regs., Part II. and the Staff Manual respectively. Title pages will be prepared in manuscript.

Place	Date	Hour	Summary of Events and Information	Remarks and references to Appendices
Bonn	25.8.19		Inspection of all Veterinary Equipment of units of the Division at DADVS Office & 42 M.V.S. Kitchen	
"	26.8.19		Usual routine	
"	27.8.19		Usual routine	
"	28.8.19		Usual routine	
"	29.8.19		Inspection of A.R. & D. Battery 161st Bgde. R.F.A. Captain Innocent reported his return to duty from the sick list	
"			Inspection of Animals received yesterday at Remounts	
"	30.8.19		Usual routine	
"	31.8.19		Usual Routine	

WAR DIARY or INTELLIGENCE SUMMARY.

(Erase heading not required.)

Army Form C. 2118.

1st Sheet A.D.V.S. Lancashire Division

Place	Date	Hour	Summary of Events and Information	Remarks and references to Appendices
Bonn	1.9.19		Usual routine	
"	2.9.19		Usual routine	
"	3.9.19		Usual routine	
"	4.9.19		Visited 575 Army Troops R.E. Kinsdorf. Inspected transport animals of 53rd Manchester Regt. Herriot. Visited the premises of Alex Wicheu Beuel where it was reported that an outbreak of mange had occurred. There is only one animal stabled on the premises which has been placed out of bounds.	
"	5.9.19		Usual routine	
"	6.9.19		Inspection of transport animals of 15th Tower Euskirchen	
"	7.9.19		Usual routine	
"	8.9.19		Visited Artillery Barracks Bonn with ref. to putting up head water troughs. Usual routine.	
"	9.9.19		Inspection B/168 Brigade R.F.A.	
"	10.9.19		Usual routine	

WAR DIARY or INTELLIGENCE SUMMARY.

Army Form C. 2118.

2nd Sheet. D.A.D.V.S. Lancashire Division

Place	Date	Hour	Summary of Events and Information	Remarks and references to Appendices
Bonn	10.9.19		Manual routine.	HWS.
"	11.9.19		Inspection of 1st Infantry Bde Hd. Qrs., 51st K.L.R., 52nd K.L.R. & 13th K.L.R. Capt. Howard R.A.V.C. proceeded on leave.	HWS.
"	12.9.19		Manual routine.	HWS.
"	13.9.19		Manual routine. Captain Meliner reported on arrival for leave.	HWS.
"	14.9.19		Manual routine.	HWS.
"	15.9.19		Inspection of animals 32nd Bn M.G.C. Frierdorf	HWS.
"	16.9.19		Manual routine.	HWS.
"	17.9.19		Manual routine.	HWS.
"	18.9.19		Inspection of animals of 92 Fd. Ambulance, 219 Fd. Cy R.E. & 90/6 Fd. Coy R.E. Capt. Lavery R.A.V.C. reported for duty	HWS.
"	19.9.19		Manual routine.	HWS.
"	20.9.19		Inspection of 2nd Infantry Bde. Hd. Qrs., 5th Border Regt. & 16th Lancashire Fusiliers	HWS.
"	21.9.19		Manual routine.	HWS.

3rd Sheet.

WAR DIARY D.A.D.V.S. Lancashire Division
or
INTELLIGENCE SUMMARY.

Army Form C. 2118.

(Erase heading not required)

Place	Date	Hour	Summary of Events and Information	Remarks and references to Appendices
Born.	22.9.19		Usual routine	L.W.S.
"	23.9.19		Usual routine	L.W.S.
"	24.9.19		Usual routine	L.W.S.
"	25.9.19		Usual routine	L.W.S.
"	26.9.19		Usual routine	L.W.S.
"	27.9.19		Inspection - animals of 3 Inf. Bde. Hd. Qrs., 57th Manchester Regt, 52nd Manchester Regt. & 3rd Manchester Regt.	L.W.S.
"	28.9.19		Usual routine	
"	29.9.19		Usual routine	
"	30.9.19		Usual routine	

L.W.Chownsupp
D.A.D.V.S. Lancashire Division

A.A. & M.S.
Lancs Div.

Herewith please find
enclosed copy of the
War Diary for the month
October 1919.

[signature]
Capt
A/DADVS Lancs Div

1st Sheet
D.A.D.V.S.
Lancashire Division
Army Form C. 2118.

WAR DIARY
or
INTELLIGENCE SUMMARY.
(Erase heading not required.)

Instructions regarding War Diaries and Intelligence Summaries are contained in F. S. Regs., Part II. and the Staff Manual respectively. Title pages will be prepared in manuscript.

Place	Date	Hour	Summary of Events and Information	Remarks and references to Appendices
Bonn	1.10.19		Usual routine	Initials
"	2.10.19		"	Initials
"	3.10.19		"	Initials
"	4.10.19		"	Initials
"	5.10.19		"	Initials
"	6.10.19		"	Initials
"	7.10.19		"	Initials
"	8.10.19		Inspection of arrival of 32 Bn. M.G.C. with A.D.V.S. X Corps.	Initials
"	9.10.19		Usual routine	Initials
"	10.10.19		"	Initials

Army Form C. 2118.

2nd Sheet

D.A.D.V.S. Lancashire Division

WAR DIARY
or
INTELLIGENCE SUMMARY.

Oct 8r 1919.

(Erase heading not required.)

Place	Date	Hour	Summary of Events and Information	Remarks and references to Appendices
Bonn	11-10-19		Usual Routine	HW
"	12-10-19		Attended meeting with A' OFFICE DIV: HQrs - to form a Committee to select animals for retention in the Units forming part of the Army of the Rhine - D.R.O. 4441 deals 12-10-19 refers to retention of the various animals - in accordance with above D.R.O. a members of the Committee selected animals.	HW
"	13-10-19		"	HW / HW
"	14-10-19		"	HW
"	15-10-19		"	HW
"	16-10-19		"	HW
"	17-10-19		"	HW
"	19-10-19		Major J.W.H. Thomas R.A.V.C. D.A.D.V.S. admitted to 36 C.C.S. Capt. H.V.M.M. Etivier O.B.E. R.A.V.C. took over duties of D.A.D.V.S.	HW
"	20-10-19		Major J.W.H. Thomas to England. As a member of Committee selected animals from Units in DIVISION for retention on Rhine.	HW

WAR DIARY
or
INTELLIGENCE SUMMARY.

(Erase heading not required.)

Army Form C. 2118.

D.A.D.V.S.
Fauna 6ix Div
October 1918.

Place	Date	Hour	Summary of Events and Information	Remarks and references to Appendices
BONN	21-10-19		Haue Roulin	
"	22-10-19		A.D.V.S & Corps inspected 41st M.V.S.	
"	23-10-19		Inspection Animals of 52nd Bn. Kings Infantry and 52nd Bn. Manchester Butt A.D.V.S X Corps.	
"	24-10-19		Inspection of 38th Brigade R.A of 62 Animals 51st + 53rd Manchesters, 206 Coy R.E, 215 Coy R.E, 32 Coy B 3 M.G. Corps.	NOU
"	25-10-19		Inspection of 1/5 Border Regiment's Animals.	
"	26-10-19		Inspection Animals belonging 6/15 Border Regiment at X Corps Animals Collecting Camp.	
"	27-10-19		Inspection of 13th Kings Infantry, 51st Kings Infantry, Divisional Train and 31st Bn. Machine Gun Corps.	
"	28-10-19		Haue Roulin Office work.	
"	29-10-19		" "	
"	30-10-19		Proceeded to Landrecy 2 miles South of Division will of No 19 V.E.S. to inspect G.S.D.V.S X Corps on the condition of the animals.	
"	31-10-19		Received altestation to Lee A.D.V.S X Corps A/Lieut Churcliff have D.V. a/D.A.D.V.S	

Army Form C. 2118.

WAR DIARY
or
INTELLIGENCE SUMMARY.
(Erase heading not required.)

/ Shiy

Instructions regarding War Diaries and Intelligence Summaries are contained in F.S. Regs., Part II. and the Staff Manual respectively. Title pages will be prepared in manuscript.

Hour, Date, Place		Summary of Events and Information	Remarks and references to Appendices
1-11-19	Bonn	Usual routine	NONE
2-11-19	Bonn	Usual routine: Called to see A.D.V.S X Corps.	NONE
3-11-19	Bonn	Inspected 206 and 219 Field Coys R.E.	NONE
4-11-19	Bonn	Visited Command Paymaster Cologne concerning Imprest Account of 42nd Mobile Vety Section	NONE
5-11-19	Bonn	No 42 Mobile Vety Section leaves this Division, was disbanded. Visited A.D.V.S X Corps to meet A.D.V.S VI Corps who took over A.D.V.S X Corps area. Inspected Remounts for Field Coys R.E. received by 206 Coy R.E. from Public City Remount Depot Cologne. On instructions from A.D.V.S VI Corps took over Veterinary Administrative duties of X Corps Horse, X Corps Animal Collecting Camp A.P.M. Bonn and 12 and 28 Heavy Batteries R.G.A. Inspected animals at X Corps Animal Collecting Camp	
6-11-19	Bonn		NONE
7-11-19	Bonn	Weekly Returns. Visited A.D.V.S VI Corps and took over Weekly Returns.	NONE

Army Form C. 2118.

2ND Ech.

WAR DIARY
or
INTELLIGENCE SUMMARY.
(Erase heading not required.)

Instructions regarding War Diaries and Intelligence Summaries are contained in F.S. Regs., Part II. and the Staff Manual respectively. Title pages will be prepared in manuscript.

A.D.V.S.
D. No. V/28/231
82/12/19
2ND DIVISION

Hour, Date, Place	Summary of Events and Information	Remarks and references to Appendices
8-11-19 Bonn	Visited No 1 Base Depot Vety Stores, Marienburg, to return Veterinary Equipment. Visited Remount Depot Cologne.	Nil
9-11-19 Bonn	Visited 121 Heavy Battery R.G.A and IX Corps Ammunition Camp.	Nil
10-11-19 Bonn	Usual routine office work.	Nil
11-11-19 Bonn	Inspected animals of 52nd & 13th Manchester Regiment.	Nil
12-11-19 Bonn	Inspected animals of 52nd D.L.I. 206, 218, 219 Field Coys R.G. and No 3 Coy Southern Divisional Train	Nil
13-11-19 Bonn	Inspected X Corps Animal Collecting Camp and 121 Heavy Battery R.G.A.	Nil
14-11-19 Bonn	Returned. Visited A.D.V.S. VI Corps.	Nil
15-11-19 Bonn	Usual Routine.	Nil
16-11-19 Bonn	Visited Plittersdorf, nr Godesberg to investigate and obtain all information about a case of Glanders in a horse belonging to Heinrich Arrival by John Stevens, Plittersdorf. A.D.V.S VI Corps Visited to a civilian interview of Dr Heidmilen civilian district Veterinary Surgeon Bonn concerning Glanders case at Plittersdorf.	Nil
17-11-19 Bonn		Nil

3rd Sheet.

Army Form C. 2118.

WAR DIARY
or
INTELLIGENCE SUMMARY.
(Erase heading not required.)

Instructions regarding War Diaries and Intelligence Summaries are contained in F.S. Regs., Part II. and the Staff Manual respectively. Title pages will be prepared in manuscript.

Hour, Date, Place	Summary of Events and Information	Remarks and references to Appendices
18-11-19 Bonn	Report on cases of Glanders at Plittersdorf forwarded to A.D.V.S. VI Corps: No British animals at present in the village.	Nil
19-11-19 Bonn	Mallein'd 19 H.D. animals belonging to 121 Heavy Battery that were one picketed in lines in Plittersdorf. 10 Coyt. Plittersdorfarea in middle of activity.	Nil
20-11-19 Bonn	Applied to 6 Divisional H.Qrs. to put Plittersdorf "Out of Bounds". D.R.O. 4529 dated 21-11-19. Cert. Chasle R.A.V.C. marching in this area to take the Veterinary Charge of Indepdt Divisional Units- called at this Office.	Nil Nil
21-11-19 Bonn	Visited A.D.V.S. VI Corps and took over Weekly Returns	Nil
22-11-19 Bonn	Visited 121 Heavy Battery, R.G.A.	Nil
23-11-19 Bonn	Inspected animals of 10 Bde. R.N. Service at Siegburg with D.A.Q.M.G. hand Division.	Nil
24-11-19 Bonn	Horse Rodeins. Office Work -. Inspected C.R.E. animals.	Nil
25-11-19 Bonn	Inspected animals A.204 & 21 Field Coys R.E. and 62nd A.T. Coy.	Nil
26-11-19 Bonn	Capt. J.B. Tate reported to Rhine Garrison from this Division for duty.	Nil

Army Form C. 2118.

WAR DIARY
or
INTELLIGENCE SUMMARY.
(Erase heading not required.)

Instructions regarding War Diaries and Intelligence Summaries are contained in F. S. Regs., Part II. and the Staff Manual respectively. Title pages will be prepared in manuscript.

Place	Date	Hour	Summary of Events and Information	Remarks and references to Appendices
Bonn	26-11-19		Inspected individual every Evacuation for Iskir Diseases and arrivals with defective vision	H.S.W.
"	27-11-19		Office work - Weekly Sanitary Returns	H.S.W.
Bonn	28-11-19		A.D.V.S. VI Corps called at this office with A.D.V.S. VI Corps 12th Army. Battery was inspected	H.S.W.
Bonn	29-11-19		Sergt Rainey (1201) transferred to 2 Sect. D.M.S. Independent Division. Mr 121 Heavy Battery and Sergt Smith A. (1092) transferred from 2 Sect D.M.S. Independent Division to 121 Heavy Battery. Authority D.V.S. 21-M.S. dated 27/11/19	H.S.W.
Bonn	30-11-19		Work & routine	H.S.W.

H.G.W. Stiven Capt
D.A.D.V.S.
32nd Division

Army Form C. 2118.

WAR DIARY
or
INTELLIGENCE SUMMARY.
(Erase heading not required.)

Instructions regarding War Diaries and Intelligence Summaries are contained in F. S. Regs., Part II. and the Staff Manual respectively. Title pages will be prepared in manuscript.

Place	Date	Hour	Summary of Events and Information	Remarks and references to Appendices
Bonn	1-12-19		Visited 121 Heavy Battery R.G.A	KW
	2-12-19		Inspected animals of M.M.P. Cav¹ Troop, 2 Squadron in Bonn.	KW
	3-12-19		Capt ANGLER took over Vet-y¹ duying charges of all units in Bonn Area.	KW
	4-12-19		Visited A.D.V.S. VI Corps at LINDENTHAL Gothastrasse	KW
	5-12-19		Visited INSTITUTE St JOSEF Bonn to see a suspected case of Glanders in a civilian horse.	KW
	6-12-19		Fulleness of Dr Freidman to the District-Vet officer concerning a case of Rabies in Mehlen and suspected case of Glanders at INSTITUTE St JOSEF. Reports to Lieut B Smyth D.A.D.V.S. VI Corps submitted.	KW
	7-12-19		D.W. Horse Eng¹ CE DADVS VI Corps. Standard Division was closed down. H.M. Stuins off¹ DADVS leave Div.	KW

www.ingramcontent.com/pod-product-compliance
Lightning Source LLC
Chambersburg PA
CBHW081409160426
43193CB00013B/2141